EFFECTIVE MEETINGS

SAGE HUMAN SERVICES GUIDES, VOLUME 17

SAGE HUMAN SERVICES GUIDES

*a series of books edited by ARMAND LAUFFER and published in coopera-
tion with the Continuing Education Program in the Human Services of the
University of Michigan School of Social Work.*

A **SAGE** HUMAN SERVICES GUIDE **17**

EFFECTIVE MEETINGS
Improving Group Decision-Making

John E. TROPMAN

with the assistance of **Bronwyn Mills**

*Published in cooperation with
the Continuing Education Program in the Human Services
of the University of Michigan School of Social Work*

SAGE PUBLICATIONS   Beverly Hills   London

For information address:

SAGE Publications, Inc.
275 South Beverly Drive
Beverly Hills, California 90212

SAGE Publications
28 Banner Street
London EC1Y 8QE, England

Printed in the United States of America

Library of Congress Cataloging in Publication Data

Tropman, John E.
  Effective meetings.

  (A Sage human services guide ; 17)
  Bibliography: p.
  1. Meetings. 2. Committees. 3. Decision-
making, Group. I. Mills, Bronwyn, joint author.
II. Title.
AS6.T73   658.4'563   80-22503
ISBN 0-8039-1520-9

FIRST PRINTING

CONTENTS

PREFACE

There are many cartoons about boards and committees, most suggesting that little gets done in them. One shows two men bending over their date books. One is saying, "Gee, if I can get in one more meeting this week I won't have to do any work!" Another, by Charles Addams, shows a father and son walking in a grove where there are statues of groups. The father is commenting, "There are no great men, my boy, only great committees." The first cartoon represents part of our feelings about decision-making groups—that they waste time, and that they accomplish little. Real "work" is not done there. The Addams cartoon, though, points out an uncomfortable truth. Group effort is necessary. There is pressure to "get on board," to "be a good team player." In spite of this pressure, we have very little information about what to do once we are on board, a situation which may contribute to committee/board incompetence and ineptitude while at the same time reinforcing their importance. This volume is aimed at helping people make that "one more committee" worthwhile for themselves and for the others there, and to facilitate the decision-making task of the group.

The central focus is boards and committees within the human-service field. In the public sphere, for example, Departments of Mental Health bring people together in decision-making and advisory roles. New efforts at localized activity are coordinated through Departments of Social Services. Area Agencies on Aging work with citizens' advisory groups in all of their decision-making activities. In the private realm, United Way agencies plan and conduct fund-raising campaigns, and when the campaigns are over, decide upon allocations. These decisions are made through—and ratified by—committees. The list could go on and on. Most of what we will say about the role of committees, the functioning of boards, and the problems they face applies to decision-making groups wherever they occur. The suggestions we will make apply to committees and boards in general.

Special thanks go to Armand Lauffer, series editor, who provided very useful feedback, and to Robert Meyers of the United Way of Canada. That organization provided partial support for an early draft of some chapters, and

Mr. Meyers made many helpful comments. Harold R. Johnson provided continual support. And finally, Elmer J. Tropman provided encouragement and wisdom.

INTRODUCTION

How often have you felt that just one more committee would push you over the edge? Most of us feel that way at one time or another. Somehow, as the opening story in the preface suggests, committees and boards seem not to "work." Work is something individuals do; attending meetings and working in groups is not work at all. And if something does get done, one may even feel guilty. There is a cartoon which shows a meeting going on, with one man bending over to another and saying, "I am enjoying this meeting so much I feel I should leave and go back to work!"

Public references, as well as cartoons, repeatedly suggest that the committee is a group of the impotent convened to do the impossible, a group that takes minutes to waste hours. In any serious consideration of problems inherent in the board and committee field, the negative view must be taken into consideration for several reasons.

One reason, of course, is to see if it is so. Are boards and committees really as incompetent as portrayed? The second reason is to determine why, despite pervasive faults, committees and boards are so omnipresent and so powerful. Perhaps there is a connection. No improvement, however small, in committee functioning and in board operation can occur unless we begin as a society to take these mechanisms of collective decision-making with some degree of seriousness. If we continue to view them as time wasting or as peripheral to the work of an organization (or, for that matter, to modern society), then we will continue to waste personal resources, "putting in time" in committee and board activity as a sort of public penance. Not much happens and we laughingly complain. If we are to take committee and board activity seriously, we'll have to find out why it is portrayed the way it is. This will give us a broader perspective from which to consider improvements.

Let's start by examining our mythology. We think of American society as having been built by rugged individualists. Boards and committees run counter to the American mythology of individualistic decision-making. The hero in the American society is the individual acting alone, deciding alone, the ruler of his or her own domain. Any social mechanism that suggests group interdependence, such as the committee, is likely to be negatively viewed for precisely this reason. Americans do not want to acknowledge situations in which interdependence with others is an important and necessary part of their lives. There are some additional important theoretical problems about this interdependence which we shall mention in a moment. For now, note that interdependence alone, as juxtaposed to independence, is enough to stimulate and maintain a large portion of the committee's negative reputation.

A second point is the ubiquity of committees and boards. It is bad enough that we should sometimes be forced to be interdependent: if we have to be interdependent everywhere, if committees and boards appear like mushrooms, sprouting at every turn, our irritation grows apace. It seems almost impossible to avoid such associations.

Interdependence and ubiquity are not the only generators of the negative image. Perhaps as powerful is the uncertainty of commitment within which one becomes enmeshed when joining a committee or a board. We all recognize there is some element of communal responsibility in group membership, yet we are often unsure what this might involve. Rural American society, for example, has long been praised for its fellowship and willingness to be helpful. The famous cup of sugar example is perhaps most often cited. One could go next door to borrow a cup of sugar from a neighbor if one happened to be out of sugar. What is less frequently observed, however, though not less frequently true, is that one was expected to pay back what one borrowed. The uncertainty involved, however, lies in exactly *how*. The borrower may feel that a cup of sugar is sufficient repayment. However, the lender may not need a cup of sugar, but rather may make some other demand on the borrower. What might be demanded, and when? Payment might be requested at an inconvenient time, or in a coin which the borrower does not wish to part with. Uncertainty clouds the horizon. The old phrase, "neither a borrower nor a lender be," seems to apply as much to the network of social obligations as it does to the simple and well-defined borrowing of money at a predetermined rate of interest. American society has always been a credit society. Social, then financial credit has been typical of us. Financial credit, of course, is preferable because the terms are well understood.

SOCIAL CREDIT

Joining a committee or board involves this fundamental uncertainty. One sits with others to make decisions. In so doing, one invariably becomes indebted to or committed to other members. It is not clear whether payment will be demanded, and, in fact, payment may be demanded in a way (through a vote or support of a proposal one would otherwise dislike) that is viewed negatively by the particular member in question. Hence, committees and boards represent a substantial amount of uncertainty to the individual members who recognize that commitments increase, that debts pile up, and that the committee and board arena is one place where they may be discharged. On the other hand, requests may be difficult or impossible to meet, thus putting a member in a very stressful position.

This stressful uncertainty may lead to the depiction of committees and boards as ineffective. Such portrayals attempt to deny, through humorous attacks, the claim they make on individuals, not in terms of the particular decision but in terms of the social obligations, the social network, the communal commitments inherent in committee and board membership. To downplay these commitments the committee is portrayed as a place where nothing gets done. Nor can anything the individual does within that context have much impact. Thus, a central—if not *the* central—reason for committee disdain lies in the reassurance such disdain gives the individual members, reassurance that they have not violated norms of independence, that if they become involved in doing something, in taking some uncomfortable action, it cannot matter anyway.

Indeed, because committees and boards can act in some way which commits or otherwise encumbers the individual members, members are restive about them. We would be the last persons to suggest that committees and boards are the absolute center of vigorous decision-making. Most of this book focuses upon ways in which such decision-making can be improved. Nonetheless, we should not ignore the reality that decisions, however poor, are made, and that these decisions involve the members in ways that intrude in other aspects of their lives. It is that intrusion, that possibility that the member might, indeed, have to defend a decision he did not like, or publicly agree with something he did not privately support, which causes discomfort within the ranks and requires a new way of thinking about committees and boards. In a sense, then, committee and board negativism tells us more about the *potential* power of committees and boards than about their impotence.

INDEPENDENCE/INTERDEPENDENCE

Negative, hostile humor about board incompetence is in part a cover for the very real demands that committees and boards make upon us. Only when we begin to recognize the importance and necessity of communal decision-making can we begin to prepare ourselves adequately for these roles. The American mythology that the individual can "go it alone" does not support the notion of training and skills for communal activity. Perhaps other societies—for example, Japanese society, where these realities are better recognized—do a better job than ours in preparing people for communal decision-making. And, indeed, it is important to understand that there is an element of psychological preparation in group decision-making in addition to the tasks and techniques. Certainly tasks and techniques, roles and rules are of high importance. Nonetheless, they are imbedded in a social-psychological frame of reference which continues to devalue mutuality in decision-making. Part of the preparation for successful committee and board activity is the realization that both individualism and collectivism, singleness and groupness have a place within modern complex society. Unfortunately for the American ethic of individualism, the need for collective activity in almost every area is increasing daily. It is imperative that we have a greater understanding about how to manage in that context.

Having said this, we reemphasize that this book is about improved decision-making. It focuses much upon improving membership skills, upon task and technique. The material can be used for training. Largely the practical outgrowth of some of the above considerations, it rests upon the conviction that mutuality in decision-making can be improved and that committees and boards can and should operate more effectively. All of us, at some point, will serve in committees, task forces, boards, and the like. Many of us will be called on to perform specific roles within them, to lead a subcommittee, serve as chair, secretary, ordinary participant. Thus, we need to know how to influence the process from a participant's point of view as well as a chair's point of view. We hope this book will serve some of these purposes. We should all know about committee management. One more committee may indeed be all we need . . . *to get the job done!*

Chapter 1

THE MODERN BOARD OR COMMITTEE

Bill Walker and Travis Smith were talking after the weekly board meeting of Bootstrap, Inc., a local voluntary agency. "I don't know why these meetings are so bad," Bill said. "Me either," said Travis. "They go on and on, and everybody seems to want to put his oar in." "It's the same on a couple of other boards that I'm on," Bill said, "They seem to be in trouble all the time." "Now that you mention it, it's the same at work too," Travis added. "My weekly production meeting never gets anything done, but we always must have it, it seems." "Still," Bill said, "we can't do it all ourselves."

In today's increasingly complex society, the modern committee is the center of decision-making activity. Almost nothing is done, no decision made, no major breakthrough accomplished, unless it is passed upon or actually created by one or more boards or committees. This is true whether within the organization or in the midst of the interorganizational network. Yet people see the committee as a pillar of ineptitude, a center of lack of progress, a group which assembles a camel in lieu of a horse. Committee humor suggests this lack of confidence. In the modern era, we face a unique and difficult situation where increasing numbers of committees and boards are set up to handle our daily business. Yet they are increasingly portrayed as incompetent. In the introduction, we have already made some suggestions concerning why this is so; now let us see what might be done about it.

EFFECTIVE DECISION-MAKING

Committees are decision-making groups. They are formed for one purpose, and one purpose only—to make decisions. There are, of course, other kinds of groups. There are social groups. There are groups that are formed for a variety of personal purposes, and these groups are, of course, legitimate. Yet we should distinguish very carefully between the functions and purposes that groups do have. Even fact-finding groups are set up to make decisions about facts. If a group is set up to make decisions, as committees and boards are, then everything done within the group should aim toward enhancing and facilitating the making of those decisions. It is to this end that we hope this guide will be of assistance.

Our perspective is somewhat different from what you'll find in other discussions on committees and boards. The most common material picks up on the difficulties in functioning that many of these groups have, and then begins to attribute them to the personalities of the members. Often cartoons depict Arthur Angry pounding the table, Silent Selma withdrawing into the corner, Turbulent Terry jumping up and down, spilling his coffee, Vigorous Victor acting decisively. These are portrayed with the hope that one can either see oneself or identify the problem people.

Implicit in this kind of analysis, and frequently explicit in the suggestions for improvement, is a series of remedies that involve shaping the personalities of such members, or failing that, removing them in some overt or subtle way. Yet after one has spent a good bit of time in the committee and board activity realm, it becomes clear that personality is less important than one initially thought. When one Arthur Angry is removed someone else takes his place. From a structural perspective, one is forced to look at the extent to which elements of the social structure may be responsible for such committee and board problems as the personalities of the members. That is the perspective that we take.

In particular, it is a roles and rules perspective. We think that if you reflect for a moment, you will realize how little education or training has been given people who assume the kinds of committee and board roles that are so common and so crucial to modern life. Typically, such information is picked up informally, usually through some kind of apprentice experience with a person whom we regard as a good chair or good committee member. There is so little teaching done that when a group of us got together and wrote a book called *The Essentials of Committee Management,* many of the publishers found themselves unable to take it seriously. One wrote back to say, "You're not seriously offering us a book on the committee, are you?" adding that his "executive committee" had rejected the manuscript.

A roles and rules perspective suggests that crucial roles are to be played within the committee framework and that frequently people have almost no idea about what these roles are—except in the most general sense—or how to play them. Typically, too, very little thought has been given to role flexibility and facility. Most of the time, we shift from one role to another as we move through the day, sometimes a chair, sometimes a member, sometimes providing staff and executive service to a group, and then back again to chair.

These changes in roles, however, are all too infrequently accompanied by actual changes in behavior. A more complete knowledge of what the roles involve and a more discerning application of them will, we feel, result in vastly enhanced committee performance. Similarly, there are a few simple rules involving the mechanics of preparation for a meeting which can immensely enhance the productivity of the meeting.

Our first point, then, is that personality is not as important as knowing one's role. The second is that the meeting itself is an end point in a long series of activities rather than the beginning point. Once the meeting begins, the course of events is largely determined by what has or has not happened before the meeting began. It is during that premeeting period that opportunities for influence and structuring exist. Once the meeting has begun it is generally too late. Our approach is compatible with a form of analysis developed by the well-known sociologist Irving Goffman. In his book, *The Presentation of Self in Everyday Life,* he takes a dramaturgical point of view. He takes Shakespeare seriously and says, "What would life be if, indeed, we were all players in a theater of sorts?" That is the perspective that we take here. The committee is seen as a play and the committee members as players. Everyone has to know his or her role and everyone has to play that role properly. There is, of course, room for improvisation. But that should occur only after the fundamentals have been mastered.

The third major point that one needs to understand in beginning to think about the modern committee is the need to make good decisions, not just decisions. All too often we are satisfied with any decision. We are so grateful when we avoid chaos and get something done that we pay little attention to whether that something is of high quality. Thus, we will be looking not only at the roles and rules of committee participation but also at the mechanics of preparation and the dynamics that emerge in the meeting itself in order to better understand the output of the committee. After all, if committees are assembled to make decisions, then the true measure of committee performance is not whether the room was well ventilated or whether the coffee arrived on time, however important these props to the setting of the committee stage are. Rather, we should look at the decision itself and ask, "Is it a good decision? Is it a poor decision? Are we possibly worse off after we made the decision than we were before the decision was made?"

RULES FOR
BOARD/COMMITTEE EFFECTIVENESS

1. know role of committee membership
2. structure on a preliminary basis
3. make good decisions

See Exercise 1 (p. 93)

BOARD/COMMITTEE FUNCTIONING

Let us now step back for a moment and recall why (or some reasons why) committees are portrayed in such a bad light. Why do they seem to have such difficulty accomplishing their purposes while, at the same time, they are of such importance to modern society? What problems must the committee cope with as it goes about its business?

Committees are typically burdened with two levels of mission. Their immediate mission is to make a set of decisions around some specific topic. However, committees serve society and their varied organizations in a much broader way. An understanding, then, of their functions is essential for a proper perspective of the modern-day committee. Functions are inherently involved in every committee, as indicated in the box below.

RULES FOR
BOARD/COMMITTEE FUNCTIONS include:

```
1. equalize participation in decision-making
2. demonstrate preference
3. represent social diversity
4. express diverse opinions
5. decide
6. influence others
```

See Exercise 2 (p. 94)

Let's examine these to gain insight on problems committees face.

1. EQUALIZING PARTICIPATION: Committees are set up to enhance quality in American life. They represent one of the subsystems of our large society where different types of people can come together; particularly where those who, perhaps, have not enjoyed the full fruits of society can begin to enter into the decision-making processes which affect them. Perhaps nowhere is this clearer than in the attempt within Johnson-era poverty programs to insist upon "maximum feasible participation of the poor." It was recognized quite broadly that those disenfranchised in one sector of the society were also those disenfranchised from the committee and the board room.

Since much of significance went on in those rooms, the planners felt that the poor and the disadvantaged should have their say. Very little, of course, was done to prepare them for these roles—new for many—but, nonetheless, the intent was to use the committee process to enhance one of the values that we cherish. This function is an important one for committees but adds difficulty to their tasks.

2. DEMONSTRATING PREFERENCE: Effective committees serve as vehicles through which the intensity of preference can be expressed. The typical way in which democracies make decisions is to vote. Even in grade school, when the teacher wants to know how many want to stay inside for recess and how many want to go outside, the students raise their hands. The majority rules. And this, of course, is well accepted. Yet the problem it presents is of a very practical nature: people are differentially affected by these decisions, and we have no good way of expressing that preference. Some people feel very strongly about a small range of issues and care very little about most of the other issues.

And yet we all get to vote on all of the issues that are set before us in the polity. This is perhaps the reason our society has developed the committee: as a mechanism by which a person's intensity of preference can be expressed. If you are particularly interested in some area and get to work on committees that work in that area, you will have, by informal agreement, greater say in what goes on. Committees, then, perform a very important function for the decision-making structure of the society, much as the outrigger on a large canoe balances the canoe. This function, too, complicates committee activity.

3. REPRESENTING DIVERSITY: Apart from equalizing participation and demonstrating preference, committees are also expected to promote pluralism. We all like to think that committees represent the full range of interests, so we will frequently try to get a man, a woman, a black, a white, a Protestant, a Catholic, a Jew, a businessman, a labor leader, somebody from uptown, somebody from downtown, somebody from the east side, somebody from the west side, and so on in order to be sure that all of the different components of the decisional framework are represented. The fact that committees are expected to have a diverse membership makes the job of decision processing more interesting, but more difficult. Decisions made by committees are sometimes faulted because the diversity of the committee is deemed insufficient. Thus, a third function links to a fourth—the expressing of diverse opinions.

4. EXPRESSING DIVERSITY: Committees are frequently seen as minilegislatures with "official" representation from the black community, women's groups, the Jewish community, and so on. This too can be problematic because the individual selected informally for these roles may not want to be "the representative." It may be that the reverend or the monseigneur or the rabbi does not want to—or cannot—speak for the Protestant community, the Catholic community, or the Jewish community, but would just like to be

regarded as a person with interests and a contribution to make. This tension between representation on the one hand and representativeness on the other becomes one of the enduring tensions of the committee.

We always seek people who can play a dual role, speak for themselves and their community. Sometimes this works; often it does not. The problem is compounded when we have knowledge that the individual definitely does not speak for the community, and yet the individual insists that she or he does. At that point, a series of complex committee maneuvers is often undertaken to supplement the view of the nonrepresentative individual so that the full range of perspectives that her or his community has can be laid before the committee.

5. DECISION-MAKING: The more complex the society, it seems, the more we expect committees to serve as vehicles for decision-making. The day of the single, heroic, organizational decision maker is probably past. There are doubtless companies and communities where single individuals still dominate. But, in the main, problems are too complex, too multifaceted. Too much information is required. There are too many implications to a particular decision for one individual to make that decision. The vigor—or lack of it—of the decision maker's personality is not the issue. Rather, it is a question of information.

How much can one person know and retain? How many implications can be processed by a single individual? How free is that individual from fatal bias? Frequently these questions are all answered in the negative. It is just not possible for an individual to be knowledgeable, or for that matter sufficiently powerful to make all necessary decisions. Thus committees come into play. Committees are designed to enable a range of knowledge or expertise to be brought to bear on a problem. One can have sitting around the table people from finance, law, the executive suite, the secretarial cadre, etc., each of whom may have a particularly crucial piece of information about a particular aspect of the decision. Singly, theirs are partial contributions; jointly, they represent the sum total of components needed to not only make a decision, but to make a good decision. Complex society is committee society whether we like it or not. But the need to have information and to have the appropriate range of information represents one of the difficulties with which committees must continually deal.

6. INFLUENCING OTHERS: Finally, committees represent, despite all of their bad press, the locus of power. Committees in communities and organizations represent the place where the formal power structure and the informal power structure get together. And if one wants to find out who is running an organization, few studies would be more productive than a study of its committee structure. There those individuals who are involved in formal decisions (to use a perspective developed by C. Wright Mills) will be found.

But also one will find those people who have Hunter's reputational authority, top organizational leaders and key organizational leaders who might not have as yet—or who just lost—a position that is suggestive of their influence.

WHY COMMITTEES DON'T ALWAYS WORK WELL

These functions, then, represent additional superordinate problems with which committees must deal. They are often a step removed from the actual apparent problem, the nitty-gritty difficulty of planning the church supper or developing a social plan for the PTA this year. And yet inherent in all committees are these other larger social duties that press upon us. It is important to have this perspective on the larger function of committees in order to understand the need we have for them in the modern era and the burdens and baggage that they carry apart from their specific missions.

These functions need to be fulfilled in one way or another, and will make work much more difficult for the committee. One must proceed with the business of the committee anyway, trying not to let such functions impede, confound, confuse, or otherwise disrupt good decision-making. It is for this reason that we stress rules and roles, because they represent a management technique through which a modicum—and, we hope, much more than a modicum—of order can be asserted with respect to committee function. Most of the time, committee competence is not what we see. We tend to see committee chaos.

Michael Cohen and James G. March suggest four reasons for this apparent chaos. They derive primarily from a lack of awareness of the essentials of committee management. Cohen and March talk about

- low salience
- high inertia
- committee overload
- decision overload

Consider some of the committees you have participated in, either as a member or chair. If things went badly, to what extent did Cohen and March's generalizations reflect the situation as you faced it? First, let's look at low salience. The bulk of committee work *is* of low salience. Decisions which are relatively trivial in nature are brought on to the agenda. Frequently, management problems within the committee lend these decisions great importance. Whether we should have square waste baskets or round waste baskets is a topic that can consume a great deal of attention. One person has reported a meeting which involved the approval of popcorn poppers for a PTA. Somebody said that they had better get a popcorn popper that would pop all the kernels because she had broken her tooth on an unpopped kernel. Another member added, "Well, it wasn't really the popper, it was really the oil," and began to suggest proper oils for popping corn. A third member then added that it wasn't really the popper or the oil, it was the corn itself, and began recommending a famous brand.

When still another individual added that it was really neither the oil nor the corn, but the heat, the meeting collapsed into committee chaos. Here was a group of community leaders, having taken time out of a busy day to do some important work, sitting around discussing how to pop corn! That kind of thing can drive even the most dedicated committee member up the wall. We therefore need to think about the ways in which items of low salience can be handled quickly and items of greater salience can be given proper attention.

Cohen and March's second point is that committees often suffer from high inertia. Like the water buffalo, they are hard to get going and hard to stop. Therefore, a set of procedures which make committee start-up easier, with particular attention to, perhaps, initial meetings, and the preparation for them, as well as ways in which committees can be terminated, is appropriate.

Third, committees become subject to overload. A self-fulfilling prophecy is created by the committee environment. The committee perceived as effective in making decisions is likely to be asked (as are individuals who are in this category) to do more. At a certain point, without proper techniques of agenda management and mission control, the committee may have more to do than it reasonably can be expected to accomplish. The result is that it may begin not to do things that people expect of it. You've probably witnessed more than one effective committee struggling under such a load that it rapidly sinks into incompetence. At that point, people—frequently the same ones who made the additional requests in the first place—point out that committees, after all, cannot do anything. But it may be too late for the committee.

Last, Cohen and March suggest that decisions tend to become "garbage cans." By this they mean that one decision can become a receptacle for all other decisions, with amendments and emendations being grafted on to something that is otherwise not terribly important. Rather than partializing the problem and using some of the techniques which will be suggested later, decisions become overloaded. The more issues and problems, of course, that are dumped into any particular decision, the less likely that decision is to be made or made well. It may have to satisfy too many people. But such problems can be solved. Committee functions can be managed and managed effectively. Quality committee decisions can be made.

It is our belief that committee performance can be vastly improved through the appropriate use of a set of committee management techniques and through the appropriate application of a set of role prescriptions. Step away with us from the simplistic diagnoses of Tommy Talkalot and Oliver Obstructionist and move with us towards making the committee a crucial decision-making group, one whose performance can be improved and efficiency enhanced.

SUMMARY

The primary aim of boards and committees is to enhance and facilitate decision-making. This is most effectively accomplished when members know their roles and when preliminary structuring has been done. Good decisions perpetuate committee effectiveness. Committee and board functions address diversity of persons, equal access to decision-making, and diversity and strength of opinions, as well as making decisions and influencing people. In attempting to correct imbalances and malfunctions in the committees we find ourselves on, it is helpful to consider the importance of our concerns, the flow of our activity, the focus of decisions and functions.

Bill and Travis continued talking. "I know what you mean, Bill," Travis offered. "Still, it seems that something ought to be done; there ought to be some way that we could improve these meetings." "Good point," said Bill. "You know, someone told me about a film he had seen, called "Meetings, Bloody Meetings."[1] Maybe we should get that film and show it. That could help. And if we gave the members a few things to read, maybe that would help too? What do you think?" "Not right away," Travis said. "We need to read a few things ourselves first. Then let's see if there are some exercises we can convince the group to try out."

NOTE

1. See the bibliography at the end of the book.

Chapter 2

TOOLS FOR EFFECTIVE DECISION-MAKING

The board of the Musical Therapy Society should have begun its meeting at 8:00. It was now 8:30, and the President was not there as yet. MTS was set up with private and public funds to plan small concerts for the homebound and institutionalized populations, as well as to take those who could not get out to musical performances. They also helped with lessons for those who needed it and could not afford it. There were many functions, and Bea Sharpe, a longtime member, was furious. Suddenly the door flew open and the President bolted in, followed by a minicam from the local television station. The President was in a state of panic. He turned to the groups and said, "The television people say that this is an open meeting, that the law says we must have open meetings. They are going to film us for the news." At that, his folder with the evening's material slipped, and the first picture the television people got was a rear end shot of the president, picking up papers which had spilled over the table and onto the floor. Bea covered her face. "Good Lord," she thought, "If orchestras played the way we have meetings, it would be chaos. Not only do we not start on time, but we wander all over the lot, we never have material on time, and often the most important items don't come until most of the people are gone. What a mess."

Perhaps the best way of looking at the committee is to conceive of it as an orchestra that comes together periodically to give certain performances for the public. When one thinks of it in this way, the amount of preparation that is required becomes more clear. Months before an orchestral performance, the score was chosen, the hall was chosen, seats were divided up, and tickets sold. Advertisements and notices were sent out, and various kinds of equipment were brought together. The orchestra members studied the score, having seen to it that they received a copy of the score; and, indeed, one of the functions of the orchestra manager is to see to it that everybody has all the copies of all of the music to be played, and is not missing a page or two in the middle of one of the symphonies. In fact, a tremendous amount of preparation has been done so that all is in readiness when the orchestra gives its actual performance.

ROLES AND PREPARATION

In particular, there has been a lot of rehearsal; people have gone over their parts individually, they have assembled in small groups and played particularly difficult sections, and they have, of course, been rehearsed by the conductor. Each of the musicians knows her or his role, as does the conductor. And this metaphor can be extended to the committee. The committee does not perform a concert, but it does perform the act of *decision-making in concert*. The chair of a committee is like the conductor of an orchestra. And it is worth stressing here that when one becomes a conductor, one gives up instrumental virtuosity. The audience does not expect the conductor to conduct for a while, then jump down into the orchestra pit, race back into the oboe section, do a little run on the oboe, jump back through the violin section, fiddle around there a bit, hit the piano on the way out, and continue to conduct. Nor does the orchestra expect the timpanist to run up from the drums, do a little conducting, then run back, boom out a few booms on the drum, then run back, do a little more conducting, and so on.

Yet our committee meetings are typically like that, sometimes with four or five conductors conducting at the same time from the same podium, with the musicians reading from different scores, or from incomplete scores so that none of them are together, with conductors running down from the podium into the orchestra, playing instruments. In fact, if we saw an orchestra perform the way many of our committees do, we would walk out. And yet we do not apply to those committees the same kind of rules that we would apply to an orchestra and expect an orchestra to follow. The key thing to keep in mind is that everybody has a set of roles to play. When you change your position, you change your role. And that has to be understood as we move about the committee orchestra.

The second point, of course, is preparation. Once the night and time of the performance have arrived, it is almost too late to do anything new or different from what has been prepared for. If one has not rehearsed, if the hall is not in readiness, if the instruments are not there, there is likely to be chaos rather than symphony. And that, too, is fairly typical of many of our committee performances. Just as an orchestral performance is governed by a score, so must a committee follow the rules if it is to move smoothly and in concert toward a decision.

We have identified five rules that help focus the committee on its task, that anchor the committee in its mission.

RULES FOR
MAINTAINING FOCUS

1. agenda integrity
2. temporal integrity
3. the rule of halves
4. the rule of thirds
5. the rule of three quarters

See Exercise 3 (p. 95)

Following these rules will be of great assistance in structuring committee activity. We'll begin with discussion of the two integrity rules.

INTEGRITY

AGENDA INTEGRITY: Agenda integrity is a simple concept, but hard to enforce. It suggests that it is the job of the chair and the duty of the committee to see to it that two things occur:

- that all items on the agenda are discussed in the meeting for which they are scheduled and

- that no items *not* on the agenda are discussed.

Although it is permissible to touch base with a new item briefly or to give less than complete attention to an older item, it is our experience that commitment to agenda integrity is necessary to insure that time and effort are properly invested. Without it, important decisions may be deferred or left unmade. Moreover, lack of integrity can take the heart out of the participants. If, for example, you stay up half the night reading the ABC report, and then come to the meeting the next day only to find that the ABC report was not to be discussed, it might be the last time that you make that kind of investment. And quite correctly. The committee has given you the message that your homework was in vain. Similarly, in school, if the teacher is not going to cover the lesson, then the student is not going to do the homework. It is as simple as that.

Many chairs and members complain that nobody reads the material that was sent out. That is, perhaps, one of the most common problems that we run into in committee counselling. And if we ask why and explore the problem a bit, we frequently hear, "I don't read it because we never discuss it," or "we never discuss it when it's scheduled," or "I was not sent the new information that makes the old material obsolete—so I wasted my time."

It is essential, therefore, for chairs and for members to stay with the agenda which is in front of them. This, of course, means that there needs to be an agenda in the first place. This point will be discussed in some detail later, but it is appropriate to indicate now that a meeting without an agenda is like an orchestra without a score. No one knows what to do, no one knows where to go. Agenda integrity is impossible without an agenda in the first place. So, as you go about committee business, insist that a fairly complete agenda be prepared and be available. Then insist that it be followed and see to it that items not on the agenda do not intrude into the meeting itself. This can usually be accomplished by an application of the rule of halves, to be discussed later.

For now, it is important to understand why we suggest so strongly that you commit yourself to agenda integrity. Most of the time, items brought before committees are complex and difficult in nature. They require information in order for a decision to be made. Typically, somebody has merely heard on the way in to the meeting that the governor's report is out. It is brought up at the meeting and people become very concerned. But, in point of fact, no one has heard the governor's report, no one knows what the governor's report says, no one knows whether it even applies in the instance. And if it does apply, no one is sure about the nature, extent, and other implications that such an application might have. Therefore, it is best not to discuss it at all. It can simply be announced, "There is a report, it has been heard, and we'll look into it." That approach, the announcement approach, recognizes the concern that late-breaking items represent, while at the same time it does not add to the agenda items about which there is no information, and for which people can only share ignorance.

The main purpose of making an agenda is to create a situation in which material can be prepared and the individual members can have the opportunity to make ready to consider the items. The late-breaking item which intrudes into the agenda disrupts that agenda, weakens the preparation people have already done, and typically creates a situation in which discussion occurs without knowledge. The fact that committee members participate in this discussion in no way changes their criticism of the committee process for spending time on such matters.

Agenda integrity, therefore, is the rule that says, "Handle those matters on the agenda; bring other matters up at other meetings." If it is a fast-breaking item, if it is a late-breaking item, it can be held over for an emergency meeting the next day. It can be handled by a small group or it can be handled, if necessary, by phone. There are alternative ways in which the item can be handled. To intrude it into an ongoing process is analogous to a situation in which the orchestra is playing along and somebody from the audience shouts out, "You know, I'd love to hear Symphony No. 40 by Mozart." The orchestra stops and begins to play it; however, since everyone does not know it, and there are no scores available, it sounds awful. And people then say, "Gee, they really did terribly on that Mozart." We have to protect ourselves against ourselves.

RULES FOR
AGENDA INTEGRITY

---

1. there is an agenda
2. all agenda items are discussed
3. items not on the agenda are
   not discussed

TEMPORAL INTEGRITY: Have you heard the story of the man running down the street who bumped into his friend? "What's your hurry?" the friend asked. "I've got to get to my psychiatrist. If I don't get there on time, he starts without me." The rule of temporal integrity is a shorthand way of saying "begin on time and end on time." Perhaps you've observed that most meetings do not begin on time and rarely end on time. Running late, we have to "catch up," cheating ourselves of the opportunity to proceed thoughtfully through an agenda. The rule of temporal integrity also suggests that some items ought to be scheduled before others and some given more time than others. Frequently, because of scheduling errors, important items are put last, and are still being considered by some members as others leave the room; perhaps as members from another committee meeting are waiting in the corridor.

Both the chair and the members have a responsibility for seeing to it that the meeting starts and finishes on time. If you do not begin on time, you encourage people to be late. It is one of the paradoxes of the modern committee that the courtesy we extend to latecomers—waiting to begin until they arrive—is the very act by which they define themselves as not being late. Lateness is defined not by the clock, but by the meeting process itself. If the process has not begun, the person is not late. With that understanding, problems of tardiness are unlikely to be changed. Our answer, therefore, to the frequently asked question, "How can we get people to come on time," is to begin on time. We should follow the rule of that psychiatrist: begin the meeting when it is supposed to begin and (even if that fails) end the meeting when it is supposed to end. A few episodes of this will convey the message to members that the meeting, in fact, will begin on time and end on time, and that this is an important factor in their deciding whether to attend.

There is a point where the concepts of agenda integrity and temporal integrity fuse. Sometimes, certain committee members cannot attend at a particular time, or at a particular meeting. Most of us have busy schedules that make it impossible to attend every meeting. We therefore rely on the agenda, the "score" of the committee orchestra, to tell us whether this is a performance that can be missed. Our judgment is based on trust; trust that what is promised on the agenda will occur when it is supposed to occur. If you see on the agenda that the ABC report is not going to be considered till the latter half of the meeting, you can leave another meeting early to make the discussion. Imagine, then, that you find that the first meeting is late in starting and that they have not gotten to the ABC report at all, nor are they likely to get to it. At that point, you feel like strangling each member of the committee, singly, and boiling them in oil, severally. Time wasting in cold blood and misallocation of time ought to be considered "misdemeanors," if not outright "felonies."

One way of protecting the integrity of agenda items is to schedule certain issues for discussion over a period of time; just as you can develop a meeting agenda, you can project agenda items over several meetings. We are referring to long-term scheduling. This simply means that by the year's end, those matters which are before the committee for that year will have been dealt with. This requires:

- preplanning
- a system of allocating agenda items to future meeting dates
- handling of assigned items at their scheduled time.

It is for this reason that agenda integrity and temporal integrity are so closely linked. If agenda integrity is violated, typically temporal integrity is also violated, and the message that these two violations give to committee members is that you are not going to seriously follow the schedule developed for the committee activity over the year. Therefore, there is not a great deal of reason to put in the kind of effort that is needed to cover agenda items. At the end of the year, when you look back to assess your accomplishments, you will find a stubble field of weeds, rocks, and only a few useful items scattered about.

RULES
FOR TEMPORAL INTEGRITY

1. see to it that your meeting
   begins on time,
2. that your meeting ends on time,
3. that the meeting keeps to its
   agenda schedule,
4. and that your committee has a
   long-range schedule

INSURING FOCUS: THE FRACTION RULES

Agenda and temporal integrity are supported by three "Fraction Rules." We call these:

- the rule of halves
- the rule of three quarters
- the rule of thirds

THE RULE OF HALVES: The rule of halves says that no item shall be entered upon the agenda unless it has been given to the person who schedules the agenda items *one half of the time between meetings.* Thus, if it is a monthly meeting, the chair or the agenda scheduler must receive the item two weeks before the next meeting. We'll give you our reasons for this rule, although by now we think you know. It takes time to organize and prioritize items on an agenda. People coming to a meeting should know in advance what they will be discussing and what decisions may be expected of them. Some items require preparation, data gathering, and study in advance of the meeting.

How often have you found this rule violated? Material relevant to that discussion is passed out at the meeting, frequently in incomplete form. We're certain you've experienced the panic of desperately skimming through the material while trying to participate in a discussion. Panic is not conducive to smooth performance. The equivalent process for an orchestra would be to pass out incomplete sections of the score as the orchestra members were walking in for the performance. Committees set the stage for panic and discord more often than not.

We would also like to suggest the elimination of a standard agenda item—approval of the agenda. We'll tell you why.

First, all committee members should have access to the agenda in advance. Typically, approval of the agenda is a parliamentary ploy which can be used to allow excluded items one more chance to be included. We feel that this is an unnecessary situation exept in the largest, mass-meeting type of endeavor. If somebody would like an item considered, it should be considered. The only thing required is that the chair be informed sufficiently early so that the he or she can look over the items and get the necessary information required by the items.

THE RULE OF THREE QUARTERS: The rule of three quarters is another checkpoint along the way to the meeting date. It requires that at the three-quarters point between meetings, the agenda be distributed along with any material required for effective preparation. In more formal meetings, this is typically called the "packet," and may involve an agenda and minutes of the previous meeting, followed by reports A, B, and C, to be discussed at the meeting. At less formal meetings, it is possible to incorporate some of the required material into the agenda.

Sending the agenda and accompanying items at the three-quarters point increases the likelihood that most participants will come to the committee meeting adequately informed. For a monthly meeting, the rule of three quarters means that at the beginning of the third week, material has to be sent out. It also means the chairs and people who staff committees can plan on a certain part of every month as a time when agenda items are coming in, and when the final pulling together of material occurs prior to sending it out.

THE RULE OF THIRDS: There are two parts to the rule of thirds. Part 1 specifies that important business be handled as much as possible within the *middle third of the meeting.* We have found that this is when the participants are likely to have most physical energy, the highest attendance, and the greatest psychological attention. Latecomers have arrived, early leavers will not have left yet. Items of lesser moment can be handled in the first third or the latter third of the meeting. Even if the meeting does start a little bit late, what one has to cut will not be as crucial.

The typical meeting is scheduled in the reverse of that order, with items of ascending importance following one upon the other until the last—and most crucial—item, which occurs close to the end of the meeting and before the usual category of new business. Since meetings typically begin late and run long, this means that the most important item is considered at the most pressured time. Undoubtedly, people will have already left. What we hoped would be balanced, reasoned discussion becomes hurried and frenetic, with only partial participation.

Part 2 of the rule of thirds suggests "breaking" at the two-thirds point, when the major business has been accomplished. Baseball recognized this with the seventh-inning stretch. If people must slip out at that point, their participation in the major items has already occurred. A break in the middle, or even before the middle, leaving the major portion of the work to be done, puts people under pressure. You've probably noticed that an all-day meeting works best when most of the agenda has been completed before lunch and people have only a few tasks to complete after their break.

SUMMARY

These five rules are essential to insuring focus and aiding decision-making in committees and boards:

(1) Agenda Integrity: all items on the agenda ARE discussed; no items NOT on the agenda are discussed;

(2) Temporal Integrity: Begin on time; end on time; and keep to a sensible internal schedule of items within the meeting;

(3) Rule of Halves: Get all items to be discussed to the agenda maker half the time between the meetings;

(4) Rule of Thirds: The agenda scheduler orders the items (she or he has them under the rule of halves) so that the most important items come in the middle third;

(5) Rule of Three Quarters: After the rule of halves and the rule of thirds, give the material; at the three-quarters point between meetings, all relevant material is sent to the members.

If applied, these will significantly improve the quality of the decision-making of any committee by strengthening the procedures which make for good decision-making. Although good decision-making does not automatically follow good procedures, it is a good deal less likely to occur without them. Decision-making on complex issues cannot take place until there is a reasonable assurance that the procedures follow the proper order and permit the disciplined and reasonable application of intelligence to those items.

Now that she was Chair of the Music Therapy Association, Bea Sharpe had the chance to correct some of the things she thought were wrong. She had worked with the group to develop a set of procedures which satisfied the Open Meetings Act for the State of Michigan, their home state. That success had brought her to the chairship. Meetings were at least beginning on time and ending close to on time. A social hour after the meeting seemed to be working well, and people looked forward to hearing a new piece, having some sherry, and visiting. They seemed to work harder during the meeting. She was beginning to be successful in getting agenda items early and making up an agenda. Things were looking up. "I just hope I don't fall flat," Bea thought as the next meeting was about to start.

Chapter 3

BECOMING A COMMITTEE MEMBER OR CHAIR

One evening the phone rings; it is a friend on the line asking you to join the ABC board. Typically, the friend will paint a reasonably rosy picture of the activities of the board, its significance to the community, and the lack of time that board involvement will take. Not having had any experience with the ABC agency, you ask a question or two concerning your lack of knowledge about the type of activity the ABC board does. Your friend may answer, "Well, that doesn't matter too much. We just focus on policy." As if policy were somehow divorced from knowing anything. Because you owe your friend a favor, you accept.

A year later, as you are reviewing your experience on the ABC board, you wish that you had not been in such an expansive mood that night. The board fights continually, no one agrees on what policy is, nobody seems to know what to do, the meetings run till late at night, sometimes after midnight, and all in all, it has been a miserable experience. Over drinks one time you mentioned this casually to your friend and expressed some mild irritation that he had been less than candid with you. His reply was an astounding one. It made you even angrier. "I just assumed you knew all of these things and I didn't have to tell you." And you began to wonder if there were not a better way.

There is.

There is a better way to *recruit* board members; a better way for *recruits to consider whether or not to accept* the invitation. And there are more effective ways of *orienting and training* recruits. All three areas are important. Together they can contribute to more effective committee participation and management. In this chapter, we will describe their effects on role performance of both committee members and committee chairs. And we will suggest a number of rules for how those roles should be performed.

RECRUITMENT

In a way, your friend was quite correct. You *should* have known about the problems on the ABC Board. The problem, of course, is that *you could not have known* without some prior experience with the organization. You were recruited at a particular moment. And that was the mistake. Recruitment is a process, not a moment. We recommend what we call "phased," rather than typically episodic recruitment. By "phased recruitment" we mean a process whereby new members are appointed or elected to committee or board membership only after some prior experience with the organization. This experience may be as a volunteer, a participant in a subcommittee, involvement in a fund-raising effort, etc. Some boards have many committees on which new prospects can "test their mettle," a bit like players in the bush leagues. Some make it to the majors; some do not. But those who do are ready to play. Some organizations establish groups like the Friends of the XYZ Agency. Such a group may meet infrequently, perhaps annually, but is briefed on a regular basis about the activities of the organization.

Their members are asked periodically to do special tasks for the board: investigating this or that, representing the board at some special function, and so on. In this way, mutual exploration helps the potential board member weigh the activities of the organization in more detail without having to make a three- or five-year commitment to board membership. Individuals in this "friends' group" may even be invited to join the board in some self-training activities, if that is seen as appropriate by the board. The board can also see whether this or that individual's interests and competencies represent the orientation desired by the board. After a suitable period, perhaps a year, the candidate can be invited to membership.

Recruitment to the board comes from an outer circle of participation which surrounds the board. It is not strangers who are brought into the "inner sanctum," but people from this in-between and/or way-station group; and recruitment comes to the "bush league" group, rather than the board.

RULES FOR
PHASED RECRUITMENT

1. identify potential candidates
2. involve them around their interests or on special tasks
3. recruit for full membership

The same procedures we use in phased recruitment to a board or committee can be used in "internal recruitment." By internal recruitment we mean the process by which officers are selected and elevated on a phased-in or graduated basis. Membership on the board is the preliminary stage, followed by a succession of posts of increasing responsibility leading to a presidency or vice-presidency. There is a great deal to be said for such conventional procedures as setting up a line of succession in which the vice-chair or chair-elect assumes the chair the following year. This assures that knowledgeable individuals are moved into key leadership roles.

CONSIDERATIONS FOR RECRUITS

Most of us tend to assume that the chair is responsible for what happens—or does not happen—in the committee. Yet that assumption ignores the member's importance and role in the committee. The chair suffers the "perils of leadership" because he or she is the front runner, the lead dog, the point person in the assignment of responsibilities. Certainly, just as the conductor of an orchestra has a crucial role to play, so does the chair of a committee. The chair has a wide range of decisions to be made that influence the course of committee activity. But we believe that the chair is not solely responsible for these decisions: the member also has essential responsibilities. And so we emphasize mutuality. The ensuing discussion provides checkpoints for both chair and member to consider before they accept either chairship or a membership.

In looking at what a candidate for the chair or a candidate for membership on a board or committee must consider, let us focus on the following.

FOUR RULES FOR
DECIDING ABOUT MEMBERSHIP

---

1. know the conditions for membership
2. be clear about the group's mandate
3. clarify the meaning of membership
4. clarify the meaning of acceptance

See Exercise 4 (p. 96)

CONDITIONS OF MEMBERSHIP: Are the conditions that accompany a chairship or membership inviting? One of the perversities of committee life is that our friends and colleagues encourage us to take positions without the authority or resources to back them up. We then get blamed when we cannot do the job. This is why both chair and member need to specify the conditions under which they will accept the position. Such conditions for the chair may include the following:

• specification of resources
• specification of staff assistance
• specification of certain kinds of membership
• limiting areas of investigation
• limiting committee responsibilities in certain areas.

For the member, conditions—usually negotiated with the chair—will focus on:

• items to be discussed
• items not to be discussed.

Also to be considered are:

• candidate's expected perspective
• demands of time and workload
• dynamics of the committee.

If these agreements cannot be made at the start, further work on the committee will probably be frustrating, if not pointless.

These suggestions represent a large order, and many of us will not be able to follow them all of the time. And, too, there are committees/boards, like community action groups, where things have run poorly in the past. It is a challenge to get these groups back on the track. The key principle here, and one which should be always kept in mind if the others cannot be used, or the conditions are not right for them, is *thinking ahead*. Think ahead about the committee/board; your reasons for being on it (one set of thoughts) and the reasons others have for wanting you to be on it (another set of thoughts). If you can keep these two perspectives in mind—what you think and what others might think—it will help place your membership in perspective.

THE MANDATE: We think all committees should have a *written* copy of their mandate, the statement of mission and role. Prospective members should have access to it. Unfortunately, these are not always available, especially if the committee is new. We strongly urge that the would-be chair get a statement in writing from the appointing authority. If this cannot be provided, the chair candidate can write to the authority after their meeting and say something like, "This is my understanding of what we discussed. Is it correct? Do you have any changes?" If no changes are made, that will do as a statement of mandate.

Doing this not only guides the chair and the member in assessing whether the job is worthwhile, but it also enables the chair to provide copies of such a statement to members. If the chair does not, members should ask for copies. If there is no statement of mandate to an already-established committee, it should be possible to abstract one from various materials, such as annual reports, previous minutes, and so on.

This mission statement becomes the basis on which a committee forms operational goals at the end of its period and assesses its performance. Mandates or mission statements are typically quite broad, and the committee will need to specify, in operational terms, how it wishes to go about the tasks it is asked to do. This often becomes the annual, semiannual, or monthly process in which goals are identified. These guide a committee in its work and provide an overall schedule of agenda items. Agendas are shaped by the will of the members and guided by the long-term mandate—mission and role—of the committee. They are also guided by the time frame required to enhance and assure goal accomplishment.

THE MEANING OF MEMBERSHIP: Those who appoint chairs are all too aware what a particular appointment means. Those who invite certain members to join a committee are also aware of the symbolic meaning of that invitation. Therefore, it is important for both chair and member to know how the public perceives their role and their appointment. A woman, for example, who will be perceived as a token must be told that this is how the public will see her, even if this information is distasteful to her, even if she does not see herself similarly. That kind of knowledge enhances role performance and clarifies actions toward the member in question that would otherwise be quite puzzling.

This type of personal analysis is extremely hard because it frequently involves seeing ourselves unpleasantly as others see us. It is for this reason that we suggest that particularly chairs—but members also—have a mentor, an individual in whom they trust, whose judgment they believe is objective and capable, to whom they can turn in situations of uncertainty and say, "What do you think? What does this mean? What does that mean?" All too often we leave chairs twisting slowly in the wind, unsure of their role, unsure of what is expected of them. When they fail to perform, we blame them for poor performance.

As part of the process of such "political" analysis, chairs and members should periodically review the committee membership. The chair should examine the list of members to see who is in the group, what they want, what their interests are, what topics they will probably push. Members should be sensitive to the role and orientation of the chair and other members because these orientations tend to shape the emerging structure of the committee. Essentially, we are suggesting the development of an "intelligence system" to generate information about the persuasions and preferences of the membership. Having "no idea that Sam P. felt this way" indicates that proper homework was not done.

ROLE ACCEPTANCE: Transition in role from member to chair or vice versa can require major shifts in orientation, and an acceptance of the constraints as well as responsibilities of the new role. For the chair, role acceptance means a shift from exclusive concern with one's own agenda to central responsibility for the agenda of the group as a whole. This point trips up many chairs. Many chairs use their position to grant and receive favors in order to advance their own fairly narrow interests. To understand how inappropriate this is, it may help to refer again to our orchestra analogy. When the chair leaves the role of virtuoso candidate and becomes conductor of the committee orchestra, he or she assumes a new role.

Chairs, like conductors, are not evaluated on the basis of whether they can make some individually brilliant contribution; rather, their evaluation comes from weighing the orchestra's—or committee's—performance under their guidance. Movement in the other direction can be just as difficult. In many situations, we recommend that a person not serve for a year on a group which she or he has just finished chairing. The role transitions can be too complex. Even if the individual can manage it, others within the group may find the transition difficult.

As it is the statesman's role which gives the chair added authority, the chair must cultivate that role, and also handle it with some care. If it becomes apparent to the committee, or even if it merely *seems* to the committee, that the chair is using the chair to further narrow personal interests, then special privileges should be withdrawn. This process is a subtle one: no horns blare; no announcement is made. The symptom is that people are less willing to follow the chair's lead, less willing to accept the chair's suggestions. Business seems to take longer, and more evidence and proof is requested. Should the chair ask about the situation in any specific instance, she or he is likely to be assured that all is well and that there just was a feeling that, in this particular instance, more was needed. This reassurance belies the facts. People no longer trust the chair.

For the member, role acceptance involves an explicit recognition of the tasks that the member hopes to perform as well as the performance most other members expect of the newcomer. If, for example, a minority member is expected to represent the minority perspective, but that member feels he/she cannot, then this issue must be faced before acceptance. Conditions must be assessed at the beginning of candidacy. It is so much easier to decline graciously at first than it is to exit later. A little homework done in advance pays great dividends as time moves on.

In addition to these rather specialized roles, there are four rather standardized roles all chairs and many committee members are expected to perform at various times.

SUBROLES

Let us now look at the major subroles of chair and member—first, the chair. The chair has four subroles:

- leader
- committee administrator
- meeting head
- official spokesperson.

LEADER: The leader sets the tone and direction of the committee. If the chair saunters in late, makes remarks such as, "Well, I don't want to be here any more than you do," engages in numerous side conversations, pokes fun at members, makes subtle racial slurs about other members, and generally presents a behavioral model which is demeaning to the committee, the committee will pick this up and act accordingly.

One aspect of leadership is the modelling of behavior. The chair informs the committee how she or he wishes the committee to run and how she or he takes the committee—lightly or seriously—by her or his actions. Actions do, in this case, speak louder than words. All too frequently we find that chairs get exactly the committees they deserve. In fact, even more to the point, chairs get the committees they ask for. Sometimes the language is body language and behavioral language rather than the spoken word. But it is, nonetheless, effective communication.

Leadership also involves political and intellectual synthesis. The chair participates a bit less than other members because the chair's contribution is more to provide mortar to join different decisional blocks than to provide the blocks themselves. On political grounds, the chair looks for possibilities for bringing about certain types of relationships among members, for suggesting new possibilities of positional compromise, for tempering the behavior of certain members, and for eliciting participation from quieter members to insure a fair balance of participation.

It is for this reason that the chair needs to be alert to what is being said, who is saying it, what are the reactions. This makes it possible to intervene in such a graceful and diplomatic way as to keep the meeting on course. If the chair has a reputation for skill in this area, she or he will be a very much sought after individual. Less stressed, but equally important, is the role of intellectual leadership.

An effective chair hears the ideas that people are communicating—or seeking to communicate—and tries to blend the idea of one member with the idea of another member. Here is the place where the chair's contribution may be directly substantive, coming up with a new amalgam that is stronger than any of the original components.

Statesmanship as it applies to leadership is a neutral evenhandedness in which no one individual or group is given preference over another, in which weaker groups are enhanced and stronger groups tempered so that every person and every group has at least an opportunity—though not necessarily an identical opportunity—to present views.

RULES FOR
A COMMITTEE LEADER

1. model committee behavior
2. synthesize political and
   intellectual material
3. preside in neutral, states-
   personly fashion

See Exercise 5 (p. 100)

COMMITTEE ADMINISTRATOR: Here the chair's responsibility is to see to it that the agenda is out and that the various rules, (particularly the rule of halves and the rule of three quarters) are followed. The chair sees that reports are ready and that people with assignments follow them up. This, perhaps, makes the chair into a bit of a nag, but if so, so be it.

Frequently, the chair interacts with people outside the meeting in order to discuss problems they are having, to provide encouragement, even to do a little work here and there. However, while it is helpful for chair to put her or his shoulder to the wheel, it is harmful in the long run to take over the task. It may be more difficult not to do it all oneself than to perform tasks members are having difficulty with. This requires restraint; it requires tolera-tion of mistakes until people realize that this chair, at least, is serious about assignments once made, and that one had better get to them.

As the meeting approaches, it is the chair's responsibility to double check the meeting room and to double check all arrangements (or to appoint someone trusted to do so). We suggest that all chairs arrive about fifteen minutes early to a meeting site to be sure that the door is open. Much time has been lost trying to find janitors to unlock a locked room or trying to find another room because, though the meeting was scheduled for room 26, someone else has already taken possession of it.

Early arrival also allows the chair to arrange the room properly, to set out refreshments or coffee, to move furniture, if needed. What this communicates to the members, then, is that the chair thinks enough of the membership to take care of details so that serious business can take priority. And it encourages members to take matters more seriously when they do not have to spend half their time rearranging furniture, getting coffee, and so on.

We have found that an oblong seating arrangement with an open center is the optimum arrangement. This highlights the chair at one end and gives everyone a clear view of fellow participants. Other arrangements, of course, are possible. A wise idea is to adjourn ten minutes earlier than scheduled. This allows time for cleanup and avoids overlap if there is yet another meeting following yours.

By preparing in advance, the chair can turn her or his attention to greeting people as they come, chatting, inquiring after this or that, perhaps doing a little work, but exchanging pleasantries as well. Frantic beginnings exhaust everyone, even before the meeting has begun.

RULES FOR
A COMMITTEE ADMINISTRATOR

1. get the agenda out
2. follow up reports
3. check on members' assignments
4. set stage for the meeting

See Exercise 6 (p. 101)

MEETING HEAD: To serve as meeting head—to, in fact, chair—is usually considered the most important of all chair roles. We disagree. While running the meeting itself is of crucial importance, of even greater importance is the preparation and role modelling that the chair provides to the committee. Running the meeting involves principally an evenhanded approach, a systematic consideration of the issues before the committee. This is where items discussed in Chapter 2 become essential. Agenda integrity and temporal integrity are crucial here. The chair does not participate in the discussion itself, but rather acts as a discussion facilitator, a clarifier, a mover, and a terminator.

If a chair feels it imperative that he or she express a point of view, this can be done by leaving the role of the chair, asking someone to express a view, or by sending the committee a note in advance of the meeting. It is not possible to press one's point of view while simultaneously acting as a facilitator, conciliator, and intellectual synthesizer.

RULES FOR
A MEETING HEAD

1. insure agenda and temporal integrity
2. facilitate and clarify discussion
3. move the discussion along
4. bring the discussion to a close

SPOKESPERSON: Someone has to speak for the committee. Often this task falls to the chair. Members generally expect the chair to pick it up and to represent the committee fairly. Among other things, this means not using the public media to slant or sway situations. The chair should give some thought to situations where public statements may be necessary, and prepare written versions in advance so that they can be checked with other members.

The chair is the first among equals in the committee membership, but only keeps that role so long as she or he acts consistently with it. If the chair begans to shirk duty, makes too many commitments, does not handle committee management tasks well, becomes a partisan rather than a statesperson, or is an inadequate spokesperson for the group, the committee will either find a substitute for the chair or deteriorate.

RULES FOR
AN OFFICIAL SPOKESPERSON

---

1. voice the committee's views, not your own
2. represent the committee's public image
3. prepare to meet the media and check your preparations with others

---

THE MEMBER

We've dealt almost exclusively with the chair. But a chair without effective membership is hardly an effective chair. What is expected of the member in all of this? The member's role is complementary with that of the chair, just as a musician has a role that complements the conductor's. The member's role involves the following:

- attention to meeting structure
- preparation for meeting content
- service to committee outside meeting
- participation in meetings
- respect for committee purposes.

ATTENTION TO STRUCTURE: It is, indeed, the member's responsibility as well as the chair's to insist upon agenda integrity and temporal integrity. Sometimes it may be necessary to insist that the agenda be followed, that previously set time lines be kept. In more desperate situations, members may need to ask that an agenda be created and time guidelines established. This is a member's prerogative. It should be unnecessary to add that the member has a responsibility to follow the agenda at the meeting. What is not always known is that members have a responsibility to aid the chair in reaching closure, even to suggest compromises when structural constraints become important.

PREPARATION FOR CONTENT: Clearly, the member must pay attention to what is there, must read the material, and be prepared for participation. Members need to have some information about the material to be discussed and to have time to look over the material and think about it. This opportunity for thought, of course, is one of the powerful reasons for the rules of agenda integrity, halves, and three quarters. If the material is not out in time, then it is not possible to look it over, and if one cannot look it over, participation is more "shooting from the lip" than anything else. However, if the material is available, as we suggest and hope, then members have an obligation to look over the material and try to have some thoughts about it and reactions to it.

SERVICE OUTSIDE THE MEETING: The member also has a responsibility to participate outside the committee in small groups interested in certain subissues. These decisions are then brought to the larger group for final ratification. A member may also act as an intelligence-gathering source, alerting the committee to troublespots, matters requiring attention, or areas where the member has particular expertise.

PARTICIPATION: This is, not surprisingly, the crucial act on the part of the member, and it is important that the member participate responsibly. Responsible membership means participating fully, yet avoiding overparticipation. Either constant intrusion into the conversation or total silence is irresponsible. Members are often unaware that the silent member is seen as the critical member. You may hear this with shock, but to be forewarned is to be forearmed. If you wish to be silent, or if you are having an off day, it is extremely useful to simply state, "I'm not going to participate as much today," thereby diffusing a potentially difficult situation. Part of the reason for this is that as time goes on, or the silent member becomes more and more dominant through her or his silence. Very simply, this dominance needs to be tempered.

The member must use some discretion and not create a situation where there are two functioning chairs; however, participation does include assistance in modifying the positions of other members, in asking for clarification and for the opinion of silent members, and engaging in some behavioral shaping of other members who are overparticipating. A member can say something like, "Steve, I think we've got your point, and I'd like to hear what Harry has to say on this issue. I know that he has some interesting perspectives." If done diplomatically, it will be an extremely effective technique because it permits the chair to support the member rather than to be always the disciplinarian, always the taskmaster.

One technique for participation which committee persons are not always aware of is what we call "remote participation." This simply involves sending a note or message to one or all members of the committee indicating what your particular preferences are with respect to a certain item (or all items) on the agenda. Obviously, this is quite handy when you anticipate missing a meeting or being absent for certain portions of it.

RESPECT FOR THE COMMITTEE: Finally, a member has the responsibility to be loyal and discreet. This means confidential committee business should not be shared with non-committee members, particularly during budget hearings, appropriation hearings, promotion hearings, or any other matters of heightened sensitivity that involve personnel or finance. Members should avoid publicly criticizing the committee, even though they may privately disagree with it or have advocated a rejected course which the committee could have used to get out of its current hot spot.

It is so tempting to say, "Well, I, of course, never wanted to do that. I was always in favor of something different." That temptation should be resisted. If a member feels strongly that an alternate direction should be pursued, it is time to resign. And resignation should really be offered in very special circumstances, not, as is too frequently the case, as a tool to secure compliance. We know those who regularly resign, who always get their way because other members fear causing a resignation. If you are a member and are faced with such a situation, propose that the resignation of that other member be accepted. It is inappropriate to keep offering to resign just for purposes of compliance.

TRAINING

The common role of both member and chair is to be sensitive to what is actually happening in the committee meeting itself and in the committee process outside the meeting. Indeed, none of these suggestions are overly striking when taken one by one, but each, if ignored, represents a major archetype of committee difficulty: the overparticipator, the underparticipator, the person who is never prepared, the person who arrives late, the person who threatens to resign, etc. Unfortunately, each of these difficulties is all too frequently perceived as a pathological manifestation of the offending member's personality.

Too rarely do we look at the operation of the committee itself and ask whether there are supports for enhancing the participation of the silent member, whether other members seek to temper the overparticipator. Generally speaking, attention to structure and to preparation for both the member and the chair pay handsomely in terms of more interesting, more fruitful meetings, meetings in which tasks are accomplished and the integrity of the individuals is retained. It is toward this goal that the chair and members should work.

However, most people do not have the background and education in group decision-making procedures because our society has not really emphasized that setting as an important one. Japanese society, for example, has paid more attention to this need. Reischauer comments, for example, as follows (1978: 188): "If the Japanese have a special decision-making process, it is the system of careful and extensive consultations before a decision is arrived at by general consensus." As contrasted to westerners, he notes that "the cooperative nature of the Japanese decision-making process makes it difficult for Japanese companies to utilize foreign executives."

American society, then, tends to ignore preparation for the variety of roles within the group decision-making process. Committee/board activity operates on a catch-as-catch-can basis. We recommend something different, a more regularized and rationalized approach to membership in decision-making groups. Typically, such activity is called "training," although the phrase "education and training" would be more appropriate, as it includes the broader aspects of perspective and understanding as well as narrower behavioral suggestions.

Let us talk about training, first noting that what follows applies equally to boards and committees. Boards simply tend to be more permanent and ongoing.[1] We want to emphasize three principles.

RULES FOR
TRAINING

1. training is a legitimate group enterprise
2. each member is entitled to support for self-development as a committee member
3. a board/committee manual is a crucial training tool

See Exercise 7 (p. 102)

LEGITIMACY: Most boards approve in their budgets an item for membership development. They expect the executive and the staff of the agency to take advantage of this to conduct professional meetings, to deliver reports about the agency's programs, etc. Yet it is very rare that the board makes any provision for such development for itself. This is because it may not conceive of itself as "needing" development. We believe nothing could be further from the truth.

Both for individual members and for a decision-making group, growth is always possible and desirable. Boards can start out with a yearly group activity which involves development, and a yearly individual activity. The whole matter of board recruitment, in fact, begins with a package of activities involving board training: both the psychological orientation to the concept that boards too can grow and develop, and the conviction that their members have a right to—and obligation to participate in—this kind of benefit.

THE RIGHT TO TRAINING AND DEVELOPMENT: Each member, then, would be entitled to apply to the agency for support for some type of activity generally related to his or her development as a board member. This is the least we can do for the voluntary service provided by many of the board members. A possibility might be meeting around a particular topic. It might be a subscription to some kind of magazine. It may be anything, as long as an appropriate, designated official approves it and there has been a preliminary OK for money in the budget for such matters.

THE BOARD MANUAL[2]: Any board also needs to give thought to the more explicit training of board/committee members. An individual who is the recruitment chair or nominating committee chair should have among her or his responsibilities the designing of a *board manual* laying out all bylaws, practices, habits, and conventions which are followed. This can be made available to new members. Such a manual can be regularly updated. It should represent more than just the bylaws and a few past minutes. Rather, it should include a codification of the way that organization, at the board level, does things. Once again, there is a curious incomplete parallelism with the organization itself.

Most organizations have something equivalent to a standard practice guide, a set of rules and procedures, a codification of policies (call it what one will) which is available through the executive director. Such a handbook or pamphlet usually details the various policies, practices, and procedures that have been approved and are current in the agency. It is also available to the staff so that both the staff and the executives can have some sense of what to expect and what rules to enforce. The board typically does not have such a pamphlet or handbook available for itself, suggesting our ambivalence toward boards and committees. At one of the crucial levels of the organization, the very decision-making level itself, people are too often left to drift this way and that, without any particular guidance.

We should like to emphasize that the creation of such a manual should not become a straightjacket inhibiting the "free spirit" of board members. In our observation, much of the so-called "free spirit" is a substitute for not knowing what to do. Guidelines, indeed, more often free us from ignorance than imprison us. Some kind of board manual should be available for every board, and it represents an important and legitimate tool for orienting new and prospective members as well as for educating existing ones. It is the type of document that one can present to someone interested in a particular board, and which can convey to that prospective, interested individual a sense of what the board is about.

SUMMARY

Here we observe the importance of graduated recruiting that emphasizes ample time to familiarize a candidate with the organization. Being a chair or a member involves being sure of the conditions of membership, of the group's mandate, of what being a member means, and of what accepting membership will mean to the individual candidate. Candidates also need to know what multiple "hats" they might wear and what subroles they might play while serving. A final point is simply that continued training and development is essential to members. As such, a board/committee manual can be invaluable. Overall, keep these points in mind:

(1) phase recruitment into your group;
(2) think through the implications of membership before accepting;
(3) remember the four roles of chair—leader, administrator, meeting head, and official spokesperson;
(4) institute and legitimize a training program.

Bill sat back and thought about his recent term as Chair of the ABC Board. His criticisms had, in the previous year, brought him to the chairship. Frank, the friend who had so inaccurately recruited him to the board in the first place, had been very angry at him for his criticism. But Frank had just left, having come over especially to congratulate him on a wonderful year as chair, and to talk about Frank's chairship of the Board Manual Subcommittee. Meetings had run well; decisions had been made promptly and had held up in ensuing months; a process of recruitment had been begun, with visitors coming to the Board to get some sense of what was happening. They had even had a retreat where they talked about goals for the future. Frank had said, "Bill, your chairship has really been an eye opener to me. I had no idea that meetings could be any different from what I knew. That book *Effective Meetings* was very helpful. I have started to use some of that stuff at work, and it is really helping!" Bill felt good.

NOTES

1. In this section, we focus upon boards because they have the resources available to begin their own education and training activities. Organizations generally, however, could institute education and training in group decision-making for all staff members,

and we would be most supportive of such a move.

2. Many organizations have board and committee manuals for the staff; most do not have them for their governing group.

Chapter 4

THE STAFFER AND THE EXECUTIVE

Sally Radcliff and Bea Sharpe were talking about Sally's recent promotion. Bea had been an executive for many years, and was experienced in working with her board and with the staff members of her agency. Additionally, Bea had had some experience with the Music Therapy Association, as chair. Bea was telling her something about the executive role in working with a board. "What's important," said Bea, "is to change a little bit from when you were a staffer to committees. Then, you did research for the group, kept the minutes, and were generally a quiet participant. Now, while you bring proposals to the group, like you did before, you can argue a bit for them." "I see," said Sally. "But I'm not really a member." "That is not true," Bea reminded her. "You are an ex officio member. That means you are a member by virtue of your executive position, but don't have a vote. This is one of the differences between your old role and your new role." "Well," said Sally, "I hope I do well." "I'm sure you will," replied Bea. "Keep in mind that you need to work with your board, let them know what is going on, develop a manual or information booklet for their use, and meet regularly with the chair. You'll do fine." "Thanks," said Sally. "I'm looking forward to it."

One of the important areas to understand in committee and board life is the role of the staff person and the executive person. By a staff person we mean an individual paid to assist the committee in carrying out its functions. We do not mean—and this has been a point of great concern to people with whom we have discussed this matter over the years—someone on the staff of the agency. Rather, it refers to the verb "to staff," to give staff service to a committee. Such a person is present at the meeting and usually has provided a range of services before the meeting begins. He or she plays a less active role at the meeting itself. This behavior is in contrast to what the executive usually does.

THE STAFFER

We'll begin by talking about the role of a staff person and then indicate how that role might be different from an executive role. The staff person is someone who is paid to assist the committee to carry out its functions. The staff person is not a member of the committee and does not have the right to participate as a committee member. This restricted role is often disliked, particularly by young staffers who feel they have a great deal to contribute and should be heard. We agree that there is a contribution to be made but do not agree that the meeting is the place for it.

Their contribution is made by working up documents for committee consideration rather than by participating in the meeting itself: this would make the line between members and nonmembers very fuzzy indeed. Members resent having a nonmember take sides when that person will not be the one to take responsibility for a favored decision. Staff persons should be unobtrusive at meetings. The staffer makes sure that the mechanics of the meeting have been handled and continue to be handled. This may require taking minutes. Minute taking in fact is the chief meeting task that a staff person is expected to perform.

BEFORE THE MEETING: There are other tasks to be performed prior to the meeting. These are grouped into a number of roles. Among these are:

- resource person
- consultant
- technician
- catalyst
- enabler
- tactician
- assistant to the chair.

What is involved in these roles? As a resource person, the staffer must be knowledgeable about areas of concern to the committee. If it is a committee on child welfare, if it is a committee dealing with employee compensation, then the staffer should be knowledgeable about that area. The committee should be able to rely on the staff person to update it about the most recent technical and professional thinking in a particular area. In this respect, the staffer is a consultant to the committee, helping the committee think through alternatives it might wish to adopt. However, this consultant role is not played directly at the meeting, but rather in submeetings or in more individual sessions where the committee as a whole is not in session.

The staffer can serve as catalyst by providing information and research findings, and sometimes through assisting the chair in bringing key individuals together whose joint perspective can open up new routes and approaches for the committee. In this respect, the staffer is an enabler, doing committee work which helps that committee function. The staffer facilitates the group process by undertaking a certain set of tasks so that the group does not have to worry about them, rather than stimulating this or that behavior within the group itself. For example, the staffer secures information, gets documents and references for committee members, takes the directions from the committee (through the chair) and follows them up. In addition, there is a whole set of housekeeping tasks such as preparing for the meeting, getting the room ready, and so on.

OPTIONS ANALYSIS

The staffer contributes primarily through options analysis rather than through intellectual or political synthesis. Options analysis involves considering the alternatives available to the committee, given present information, and presenting them in an order that promotes committee discussion. At this point, we strongly suggest that the staffer put these options in writing. When that is done, the staffer can—and should—add her or his own recommendations (as long as they are clearly distinguished from the options). One of the major problems that staffers have, and hence committees have with staffers, is that their own views get mixed up with the analyses they are presenting. This makes it impossible for the committee to sift out a set of alternatives not colored by a staffer's often unconscious views. Our suggestion is to make those views conscious by including them in the options memo.

Staffers should practice doing policy options, which we recommend be three-part memos composed as follows: problem analysis, presentation of alternative solutions, staff recommendations.

RULES FOR
AN OPTIONS MEMO

1. analyze the problem
2. present alternative solutions
3. offer staff recommendations

See Exercise 8 (p. 103)

In this scheme, both alternative solutions and staff recommendations are clearly identified. It is here, in the written recommendations to the committee, rather than in the committee meeting itself, that the staffer's knowledge makes a direct contribution.

DEVELOPING STRATEGIES

The effective staffer collaborates with the chair as a strategist and tactician. Since agenda items need to be ordered from easy to difficult to easy, a preliminary ranking must be done by the staffer.[1] The order can then be readjusted or changed by the chair when the two meet. Indeed, it is important that the staffer meet regularly with the chair before meetings, particularly if there are issues pending about which the two might disagree.[2] Such disagreements can be fully and completely discussed in a private meeting, though they may not be resolved there, but should not go on in the meeting. It confuses members to be forced to sit through a detailed, in-depth discussion between staff and chair about this or that. Such discussion should occur outside the meeting or in special submeetings.

In working with and assisting the chair, the staff person is responsible for helping to develop meeting tactics. The staffer may:

- suggest ways to handle items in terms of order and content
- name key interested individuals whose views need to be considered
- point out opponents, if known, to a particular direction.

These tasks complement the staffer's responsibility to work with the chair on committee strategy. Together, the staffer and committee:

- plan agenda items ahead (for future meetings)
- develop a fund of knowledge about items of committee interest
- represent views of other committees/individuals to the committee.

Because staffers know a good deal about what is going on in both the community and the agency, they are in a good position to suggest that certain items be hastened or held back. Decisions by this committee, for example, may serve as the basis of deliberations coming up in another committee. It may be more appropriate for Committee X (the program committee) to wait until Committee Y (the finance committee) has acted before it spends a lot of time discussing programs for which there may be no budget. Committee members and chairs would do well to make effective use of staffers.

STAGE MANAGING

After meeting with the chair, the staff person is responsible, usually at the chair's direction, for the details of meeting preparation. Many of these responsibilities would be those of the chair were there no staff person. For example, making sure the room is ready, sending announcements out, arranging for parking, ordering refreshments can be delegated to staffers if they are available. This is not always the case. Committee and board members must be careful not to misuse or abuse staff members whose contributions in other areas may be more important.

Typically, however, when a staff person is available, it is her or his responsibility to perform many of the stage management aspects of preparation for meetings. But when the meeting itself becomes a reality, the staff person "lies back," playing a subordinate role, taking minutes, and contributing on request. He or she may be more assertive when clarification is needed. If there is a clear point of fact, the staffer must mention it with care. However, the staffer should heed the spirit of this recommendation rather than its letter. Sometimes staffers can participate a bit more, if the occasion seems to call for it. However, if a staffer looks over his or her behavior within a given period and notices a pattern of increased participation, it may be time to cut back. The tendency to participate like a full member and even to usurp the role of the chair must be resisted.

POLICY LOYALTY

Like committee members, the staff person is responsible for "policy loyalty." But he or she is also responsible for contributing beyond simple compliance with the goals and missions of the committee. If the chair does not get that kind of support from a staff person, both chair and staffer may find themselves seeking other assignments. To the chair, a nonsupportive staffer represents a potentially lackluster performance at best and dangerous sabotage at worst. Staff persons are no more comfortable with a nonproductive role. It is difficult to continue to do something that you feel is in contradiction to your own policy orientations. However, until this point is reached, the staff person should not be critical of the committee for which he or she works, except in discussions with her or his administrative superior. That is the correct route by which to raise questions about committee activity. We are frequently asked to carry out missions with which we disagree. If such disagreement is less than fundamental, then a talk with the chair about the ways in which one might carry out the mission in question becomes appropriate.

BOUNDARIES OF SERVICE

We have stressed that the staffer needs to develop a good working relationship with the chair. To this end, an early meeting with the chair, before accepting a staff role, can be very useful. This meeting could, of course, be initiated by the chair, but it is generally the staff person who is expected to take the initiative. If it seems that there will be serious strain working with a particular chair, that potential difficulty should be brought to the attention of the appointing authority.

Strains are bound to occur from time to time because staffers typically have two sets of bosses. One is the staffer's administrative supervisor, usually the organizational superior and the person who assigns the staffer to the particular committee. The committee chair usually has authority over the staff person and can direct that person's work and effort for the time the staffer has available.

This brings up an important matter. The amount of time available should be decided upon as much as possible before staff work begins. Are we talking about one day a week, two days a week, three days a week, full time, or what, exactly? Committee work can mushroom: we have been involved in many situations where staffers have been desperately overburdened but have felt powerless to pull out of the situation, short of quitting and finding another job. The pressures that can lead to resigning typically derive from conflicts concerning how much time is needed versus how much time is available.

When the time needed exceeds the time available, then the staff person should have a frank discussion with the chair, indicate what his or her limitations are, and think through with the chair how additional resources might be garnered. If the issues can not be resolved here, the appointing authority must be consulted. The staff role can demand much time and effort. It is not made any easier by the fact that a staffer may simultaneously hold two or three assignments with two or three committees and have two or three chairs to work with, each of whom has a somewhat different style of working. Given such a situation, staffers must keep the work related to each committee as separate as possible to avoid overlapping.

RULES FOR
STAFFERS

1. inform/provide consultation
2. give technical assistance
3. stimulate committee activity
4. promote committee function
5. analyze choices
6. develop strategies
7. set meeting stage
8. serve committee interests

See Exercise 9 (p. 104)

THE EXECUTIVE

The executive is a kind of high-level staff person. However, while the executive shares many responsibilities with the staff person, there is a fundamental difference. Executives typically work with boards of directors. Their responsibilities are with the central policy-making body of their organizations, while staffers may assist a whole range of committees, including a board *and* a variety of subcommittees. Executives typically have one central responsibility—to "their board."

The superintendent of schools plays this role with respect to the board of education. The executive director of a family-service agency plays this role with respect to the board of the agency. Someone who is director of a mental health clinic is the executive to the board, which hires and fires him. The executive director is an individual who has primary responsibility to a policy-making board rather than to committees. Committees may recommend policy, but may not always have policy-making authority. This makes interaction with boards potentially more serious, and of greater consequence, than is typically the case with committees and subcommittees.

POLICY AND ADMINISTRATION

More important, an executive shares responsibility for the mission and role of the agency or organization. Thus, he or she is usually a member of the board in an ex officio or nonvoting capacity. This pattern of having an executive in a nonvoting capacity is not typical of all sectors. Indeed, one of the powers of the "chairman" came from the fact that the chairman was also chief operating officer. This is true, for example, at the University of Michigan, where the president of the University is also the chief operating officer of that University. Large corporations tend to use this pattern as well.

In human services, we are more familiar with the separation of the board and the executive, with the board tending toward volunteer or lay representation of community interests and the executive being the highest-paid professional staff person within the organization. These differences in orientation, background, and overall responsibility can generate conflict. It is part of the executive's responsibility to be aware of these potentials and to work to avoid them.

The old distinction between administration and policy is probably not fully applicable. It suggests that the board makes policy and the executive carries it out. The truth lies more in an amalgam than a distinction. The board *with the executive* makes policy and the executive carries it out. The executive also makes policy without the board. In fact, added to differences in background and responsibility, the fuzziness between policy and administration continually creates difficulties and tensions between board and executive.

It is not possible to clarify these differences completely. In part, that is because there is a jointness about the responsibility. The executive, after all, is the one who must carry out the policy decisions. She or he will need the support of the board, and the board will need the support of the person in that slot.

DUTIES AND ROLES

What, then, are the duties and the role of the executive? We have identified seven:

- professional presentation
- alerting the board to policy issues
- making a case
- working with the board as a partner
- developing and educating the board
- dealing with board sensitivities
- working with staff on behalf of the board.

We will comment on each of these.

PROFESSIONAL PRESENTATION: This involves the board's expectation that the executive is a knowledgeable, up-to-date professional in her or his chosen field. The executive's duty is broader and more inclusive than the similar responsibility of a staff person. The executive is seen as the professional custodian of the agency and the person who will answer professional questions asked by the board. For this reason, the executive must be alert to professional issues and be ready to educate the board in regard to these as time goes on. Stemming from this professional competence is the second role—alerting the board to policy issues.

POLICY ISSUES: While members of the board and the chair will know of emerging policy issues in the community, the executive is thought to be the key in this function. Like the chair, the executive must develop an intelligence system that brings community issues, staff issues, and issues affecting the agency to his or her attention and then to the board for consideration and action. Similarly, in professional matters, the executive is expected to alert the board to matters of interest developing in the field. New techniques of intervention, for example, new techniques of bookkeeping, new standards, new regulations from federal, state, local or other sources of review are part of the kind of information that the executive brings to a human-services board. MAKING A CASE: The executive is expected to—and entitled to—make a case. The authority and expectation stem from the executive's presumed expertise.

WORKING WITH THE BOARD AS A PARTNER: The executive works with the board in partnership as a colleague who shares with board members in the interests of the organization. This is because the executive and board share "custody" of the organization's mission and role.

Though it hires and fires the executive and approves her or his salary, the board hardly regards the executive as just another employee. The board and executive share a tenure which the executive must cultivate. The board sees and must respect the fact that the executive has a longer term, perhaps, than many board members. Thus, the executive may have a perspective of history as well as a professional competence. Nevertheless, the executive must accept the fact that the board can go against his or her wishes. Joint responsibility does not mean that things always have to go the executive's way.

DEVELOPING AND EDUCATION: A special responsibility of the executive is to engage in a process of board development and education. We recommend a minimum of a training session once a year; what some organizations call an "educational day" for board members. This can help boards and executives (and fellow board members) get to know each other better. Here new materials about the mission and role of the agency can be shared. A set of such materials could be discussed here. Think of how little opportunity there is for board members—as opposed to staff—to meet to discuss their developmental needs. We urge boards to take the initiative, if their executives do not, to allocate some small portion of their resources to a board development fund. Confer with the executive on how this fund might be generated or allocated. Consider also special sessions for new members in which they are oriented to board member responsibilities.

DEALING WITH BOARD SENSITIVITIES: In the human-service field at least, board activites are volunteer contributions. People participate on boards out of a sense of public commitment, public interest, and concern for a particular area. Executives must recognize that this volunteer aspect requires some attention; particularly when the executive has had the job for a long period of time, she or he may come to regard the board as an obstacle. This attitude violates the central principle of mission sharing. When either the executive or the board believes that only he or she or only the board has full responsibility, a good working relationship is hampered.

Because we expect that the executive will know more about these matters than the board, we feel it is the executive's responsibility to be tuned to board sensitivities. For example, executives commonly have stationery designed to feature their names prominently and the board's name in smaller letters, if at all. Lettering should be equal, or if anything, out of courtesy the board's name should be printed in slightly larger type. Trivial as this example is, it represents an attitude, a disposition that executives sometimes take toward the board.

Rather than working with the board and educating it, some executives believe the board is to be overcome. And to be sure, there are times when such effort is necessary. But all too frequently this perspective is arrived at out of frustration because other kinds of working relationships were never established. Where working relationships are well tended and cultivated by the executive, a mutuality and sense of jointness is much more typical.

The executive is also responsible for many of the mechanics of meeting preparation. All too frequently we find executives grasping for more exalted responsibilities and turning those which appear less elegant over to clumsy and uninterested subordinates. Thus, matters of the agenda, the room, the meeting time, getting packets out may be handled in a lack and unimaginative fashion. Board members may feel slighted, unappreciated. Though they may be silent about their feelings, tensions can be expressed more appropriately in other kinds of board decisions made. Therefore, in any problem between executive and board, we look first at the staffer's role played by the executive (though an executive *does not* take minutes) to see whether or not it is being handled appropriately, even though she or he frequently reviews minutes for accuracy and policy appropriateness. Then we move to the larger and more complex duties.

WORKING WITH STAFF: The executive is the working liaison between board and agency staff. The executive has to interpret board policy to the staff and has to vigorously interpret staff action to the board. This may be a hot spot for the executive, as he or she becomes disliked for a moment by both staff and board. However, that triad needs to be cultivated. One of the best uses of a once-a-year educational or training session is to provide opportunities for interaction between board and agency staff. Board and agency staff, at meetings orchestrated by the executive, can be helped to share perspectives and concerns. It is frequently quite a surprise for each group to hear what the concerns of the other group are. Boards, for example, often feel that staffers are not committed and are just "out for the busk." Staffers, for another example, often feel that boards are removed and remote, that they don't really care. These perceptions are often wrong on both counts, and can damage the development of a relationship of trust.

RULES FOR
THE EXECUTIVE

1. present professional perspective
2. offer expertise where needed
3. keep board informed of policy issues
4. work sensitively with board
5. offer development opportunities
6. work energetically with agency
   staff and link board to staff

SUMMARY

Staffer roles and executive roles are difficult and different ones. The staffer needs to provide a supportive service to the board or committee, often playing a subdominant role with respect to participation in the meeting, stressing the facets of participation and preparation. Executives, on the other hand, are almost always working with decision-making boards or decision-making groups. This gives their job a somewhat different character, although they do play (with the exception of taking minutes in the meeting itself) the staffer role. There is a jointness to the decision-making functions which occur here, even if the executive does not have a vote. The board has hired that executive to provide professional guidance and perspective. His or her views will be taken into account. When that relationship begins to break down, good decision-making becomes very difficult.

As Bill Jones left the meeting of the Helping Friends Board he was stunned. Fired! He never thought it could happen to him. Anger rushed over him, driving away the waves of anxiety that competed for his feelings. He could not really think straight. But he remembered a conversation over lunch a few weeks ago with Bea Sharpe. She had indicated that, informally, she had heard some of his board members were displeased with him, felt that he was moving too fast, not bringing them information. Bill recalled replying that boards bored him stiff and indicating that he was the one responsible for moving the agency ahead. Bea had cautioned him that sometimes a good working relationship with a board pays off. He recalled telling her how fired up he was about some new plan. Now he was actually fired. Perhaps he should call her back and see what he should do . . .

NOTES

1. See the chapter on the agenda for more information on this system.

2. It is in the private meeting with the chair that the staffer expresses disagreement. In the final analysis, however, the staffer should go along with the decision of the chair in terms of approaching a particular matter.

Chapter 5

THE AGENDA

Hank left his fourth meeting of the day, the Social Planning Committee, feeling foul. As a local mental health executive, he had to attend more meetings—and was on more committees and boards—than almost anyone he knew. And the damn meetings were so unproductive. This last one in particular made his blood boil. No one had prepared anything, and everyone threw out different topics, problems, and solutions. No one, it seemed, had taken the time to put things together. He had asked for an agenda. The chair had said, "Good. That's the first item—the agenda." At that point, Hank had said, "Look, you folks. If you can't be better organized than this, I have got better things to do with my time." Then he left, while Bob Grey muttered something about "compulsive" types who want to stifle creativity. As he went out the door, Hank thought, "That's not creativity, that's chaos."

THE AGENDA

The agenda defines the purpose of a meeting. It relates that purpose to the larger mission and the role of the organization. Available to chair, members, staff, and executives, it is more than a list of topics. It is a substantive document which informs the members, as well as other interested persons, about how and when the committee will make its decisions. Why, then, is the agenda so often glossed over? Typically, it is written a few minutes before the meeting, perhaps even at the meeting. Topics are listed with no regard for the information needed to consider the issues intelligently. This is, of course, not always the case. Topics listed in crude order are often sent out in advance of the meeting, but these all too frequently are not adequate to provide the guidance needed for preparation. In a word, they are not "functional."

Before describing the frame of a functional agenda, we will look at the typical order of events at business meetings. We'll then spell out both what an agenda should be and can be. Along the way, we will suggest a set of rules to follow that will help shape and structure the meeting.

THE MINUTES AND HOW THEY ARE DISCUSSED

The typical meeting begins with a review of the minutes of the previous meeting. Minutes summarize what occurred at that meeting. Properly written, they record all decisions made. If their accuracy is challenged, the review of the minutes not infrequently becomes the occasion for discussing last week's or last month's meeting all over again. This is especially true if the minute taker has attempted to present in depth what people said instead of what they decided. A tremendous amount of time is wasted on discussion of the minutes. To help you avoid the stretching out of the minutes "into hours," we suggest the focus be on content, not process, except in that unusual situation where legal requirements dictate process minutes. By process minutes we mean minutes whose structure is a verbatim—or very close to verbatim—record. Content minutes, on the other hand, represent an intelligent summary of the points of view expressed on a particular issue, without names attached. Review of the discussion is followed by the conclusion or decision made. The substance of the debate must be reflected, but every side comment, joke, and irrelevancy that crept into the discussion should be ruthlessly rooted out. Emphasize the key points; highlight them, don't hide them.

We recommend you learn to use what we call "agenda-relevant" minutes. Agenda-relevant minutes are a form of content minutes in which the headings in the agenda are repeated in the minutes. With them, anyone can look at a copy of the agenda for the meeting of January 12, then at a copy of the minutes for January 12, and see topic identifications and find out what happened at the January 12 meeting. If the ABC report was discussed, the minutes explicitly identify the ABC report, record the discussion about it, and note the decision or action taken.

RULES FOR
AGENDA-RELEVANT MINUTES

---

1. report views without naming disputants
2. summarize debate
3. record action taken
4. categorize items under agenda headings
   of the previous meeting

See Exercise 11 (p. 106)

REPORTS: HOW THEY ARE MADE AND DISCUSSED

Many groups follow approval of the minutes with an extensive series of reports. One PTA that we have served on has sixteen subcommittee reports always listed in the agenda, whether or not there is to be any report made. Unfortunately, finding the subcommittee listed may induce some subcommittee chairs to make some kind of a report—any kind. This is extremely time consuming: people will make reports even if they have nothing to say, and they frequently will take the occasion to add something, which is then picked up by another individual—and off the meeting goes. We recommend that the entire process of giving reports be stopped. This may seem extreme. It isn't. If the chair checks with subcommittee chairs sometime before the halfway point between meetings, it should not be difficult to find out if there is something to report, and if so, what. Only those items requiring action or providing other committees with information that can help them out should be listed on the agenda. They should be listed in such a way as to communicate to the reader what action is invited. Instead of listing "the ABC report" on the agenda, include notes with each item that suggests that action should be taken. For example: "Consideration of the ABC Report," "Approval of School Bus purchase," "Ratification of the Budget," "Hiring of the New Executive," and so on. Communicating the invited action in the language of the agenda will go a long way toward informing members in advance of the meeting what it is they are being asked to do. It is also likely to encourage them to read committee reports before the meeting. That's where they belong—before, not during, the meeting.

Reports given verbally are one of the greatest time wasters with which committees must cope. If there is no action coming from the report, a summary report, in writing, can be attached as an appendix to the minutes and agenda that go out in the member's packet. It is much easier to scan a paragraph than to listen to a paragraph. Oral paragraphs tend to expand and expand. Shaving the agenda down to action items communicates an action-oriented message to the membership. If your group must have reports, put them at the end, in the last third of the meeting, after action has been taken on the crucial items.

The rule of halves, you will recall, specifies that the chair or staffer call subcommittee people to inquire about their reports. If one meets monthly, then a call toward the beginning of the second week not only secures information, but prods the individual to get cracking. There should be sufficient time between the call and the meeting to handle problems. But if they cannot be handled, the report may focus on the problem itself, which then becomes an item of business.

We further recommend that the scheduled reports not be sent out in their entirety. Perhaps the greatest single complaint from members, from staff, and from chairs about the committee and board process is about volumes of paper produced and not read. Part of the reason that people do not read reports is that they have only a 50 percent likelihood of being discussed at the meeting. However, a contributing reason may be found in the bulk of the report itself. This is why we feel it is much better to prepare an "executive summary" of long and detailed reports. This:

- limits material to a one- or two-page digest
- highlights key issues
- links material to major report by reference notes.

Good executive summaries need not be longer than 10 percent of the original document. If effectively written, they may stimulate members to ask for the full report. A report requested by a member is likely to be read more carefully. What should go out with the agenda, then, is not a thick wad of reports, but a thin packet of executive summaries. People who are pressed for time and who never read a full report often glance fairly systematically at the executive summary.

RULES FOR HANDLING REPORTS

1. list only relevant reports
2. note expected activity
3. summarize reports requiring no action
4. send executive summaries of scheduled reports

Remember the rule of halves for agenda inclusion and the rule of thirds for item placement: get items in by half time; put key items in the middle of the agenda. Finally, at the three-quarters mark—the rule of three quarters—the agenda must go out.

NEW STRUCTURE

We do not recommend the typical agenda of minutes, reports, old business, new business, and then miscellaneous business. What type of structure do we recommend instead? We recommend a bell-curve structure. In a bell-curve structure, items of the simple sort come before items of the difficult sort. The most difficult item should appear just past the middle, followed by simpler items toward the end of the meeting.

As noted elsewhere, it is imperative that the agenda maker link the agenda structure to the clock so that one can take advantage of the psychological, physiological, and personal energies and presence of key individuals.

In the bell-curve structure, we try to plan for seven types of items to be covered in a two-hour period. If necessary, this can be stretched to a third hour. Three hours seems to be about the maximum time people can meet without a significant break. We think that people who swear to meet all night if necessary should be ignored. It is simply not possible to meet productively for such an extended period of time. Beyond the three-hour point, people will often do anything to adjourn.

What are the seven items that provide the frame, the structure for the bell-shaped agenda? We've listed them below as a set of rules for framing effective and efficient meetings.

RULES FOR
FRAMING THE MEETING

1. enter brief, agenda-relevant minutes
2. make informative announcements
3. decide on less controversial items
4. consider most difficult item
5. break
6. talk over FDO (for discussion only) items
7. consider the least difficult item(s) and
   call for adjournment.

MINUTES: If the suggestions we made are followed, these should be crisp and relatively brief minutes, focusing on content and decision, which are explicitly linked to the agenda of the previous meeting. Follow this procedure and controversy over the minutes should be reduced, if not eliminated. Accuracy is all that should concern members. It is proper at this point to approve minutes or to correct inaccuracies. To keep members from using the minutes to rehash last week's discussion, the chair should ask those who wish to discuss the minutes to suggest the "language they feel would be more appropriate." This focus on language tends to temper the tendency to use the minutes as a springboard for fresh discussion.

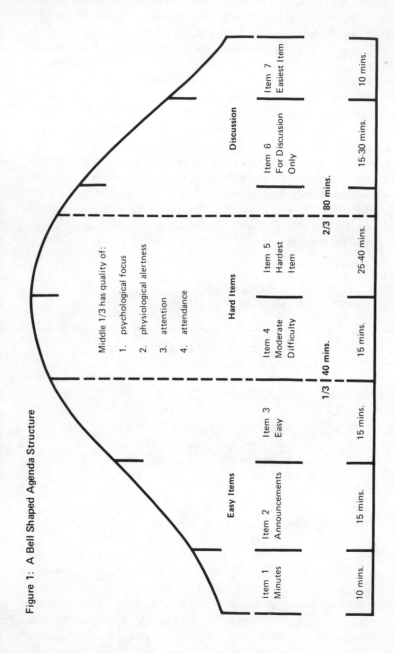

Figure 1: A Bell Shaped Agenda Structure

Middle 1/3 has quality of:
1. psychological focus
2. physiological alertness
3. attention
4. attendance

Easy Items			Hard Items		Discussion	
item 1 Minutes	Item 2 Announcements	Item 3 Easy	Item 4 Moderate Difficulty	Item 5 Hardest Item	Item 6 For Discussion Only	Item 7 Easiest Item
10 mins.	15 mins.	15 mins.	15 mins.	25-40 mins.	15-30 mins.	10 mins.

1/3 | 40 mins.   2/3 | 80 mins.

2 Hour Meeting = 120 Minutes

ANNOUNCEMENTS: This category is a flexible one which can be used to fill in some time if, in fact, the meeting had to begin with few people. It is essential that the meeting begin on time. Making announcements early—before decisions have to be made—respects those members who arrived on time and defines anyone who arrives afterwards as late. Announcements are declarative, noncontroversial, and informative in nature. Discussion should be kept to a minimum. If an item provokes great discussion, then it should have been a regular agenda item. It can be placed on the next meeting's agenda.

LESS CONTROVERSIAL ITEMS

Less controversial or easier-to-handle decision items should appear early in the agenda. We prefer to arrange items in order of increasing difficulty. Once the first decision has been made, participants feel freer, more confident that they can dispose of more difficult items. Notice what we have done so far. The meeting has begun on time, and we have moved quite rapidly into a decision-making frame of mind. The very first activity led to a decision—approval of the minutes. There was then a brief pause for announcements, followed by decisions or actions on several less difficult items.

By now, we should have completed approximately the first third of the meeting. The agenda has been written in such a way as to specify exactly what the decision desired is: approval of the minutes, appointment of the new executive director, etc. People who read the agenda when they receive their packet know exactly what is asked of them. In this way, the agenda becomes a tool for shaping the meeting. It informs and shapes the behavior of members even in advance of their attendance.

THE MOST DIFFICULT ITEM: At that point, the agenda scheduler marks down another item. It occupies the middle section of the meeting. It is put there to take advantage of peak attendance. Latecomers will have arrived, and those making early departures will not yet have left. This location also capitalizes on psychological energy. It follows completed decisions which have made people feel good about their decision-making ability. Because they are not stuck at the end of the meeting, people will not have to consider key items as they are leaving the room. Giving ample time—usually half an hour to forty minutes for discussion of a difficult item—increases the likelihood that it will be properly dealt with. If a decision is not reached in about forty minutes, then additional work has to be done. Perhaps more information is needed. Perhaps the item should be tabled and brought back again. When that happens, it is perhaps unfortunate, but there may still be room to complete a bit more business. But the committee has worked hard, and it is time for a break.

BREAK: Following the rule of thirds, we should be at the end of "Item Four," approximately two-thirds of the way through the meeting. Two types of breaks may be considered. A brief stretch break sometimes helps. The chair might permit people to get up, walk around a little bit, shake themselves down. This not only provides physical relief, but also defuses whatever animosities have been built up during the discussion of the difficult items that preceded the break. A five-minute stretch can do a lot of good, but it may not be enough. The members have had a break. The meeting process needs to break as well. That's why we suggest the FDO item.

FDO ITEM: FDO, the "for discussion only" items, further help to release tensions. Members are informed in advance through its location on the agenda that no decision is going to be taken on this item. It does more. Too often decisions are made prematurely, especially if there is a proposal for action before the group prior to adequate discussion.

When committees develop a habit of putting FDO items on the agenda, members look forward to discussions without decisions staring them in the face. For discussion only items provide an opportunity for the ventilation of feelings, for the assessment of political orientations. It gives chair, staff, and members an opportunity to survey the lie of the land. It sets the stage for compromises that can be made between meetings. The release of pressure at one meeting followed by opportunities for reassessment and for working out differences permits members to get down to business when the items comes back on the agenda at the following meeting.

Two techniques of handling "for discussion only" items contribute to better decisions at the next meeting:

• the "straw-vote" technique, and

• the "in-principle" technique.

When the chair asks for preliminary indications, on a straw-vote basis, of which series of discussed alternatives might be preferred, it helps the staff to avoid wasting time in research on a particular issue or option that no one wanted anyway. This technique helps prioritize options so that the staff can focus its time most appropriately.

The in-principle technique—useful for other items as well—separates the "gut element" in a decision from lesser "how-to" aspects.[1] Thus, a board can favor one type of action over another. Once that "in-principle" decision is established or the "in-principle" orientation is known, it is possible to work out relevant options, avoiding matters of lesser interest. It also helps discussion to stick to the largest issue in principle or to details. Some discussions go from large principles to small details, and we call this "discussion oscillation." It is extremely difficult to participate in such a discussion because you are never sure at what level the issue is seen at any given moment.

THE LEAST DIFFICULT ITEM: We think it is always a good idea to end the meeting on a positive note, one of agreement and accomplishment. About

80 percent of the way through the meeting, the chair says that it is time to finish with a brief discussion of the last item or items—quickies that can be dispatched with ease. The psychological value of dispatching several items with ease is great, especially if the discussion up to that point has been difficult or outcomes problematic. This permits people to leave with a sense of orderliness; some sense of accomplishment. This is the point at which the meeting should be adjourned.

The end of this week's meeting is the beginning of next week's meeting. Therefore, the psychological frame of mind, the social conditions of the meeting as it ends, for the person and for the group, are important determinants of whether someone will make the effort to come next week.

This agenda framework is quite different from the typical agenda framework that one sees. It requires preplanning and judgment on the part of the agenda maker. Items must be located in appropriate ascending and descending order. It requires structuring the agenda in relationship to the clock so that one can cover the items in the time available. If it appears that there are too many items, then more meetings are necessary. That is an alternative we recommend over extending meetings for ever longer and longer periods.

SUMMARY

Proper attention to the agenda and its use as a central tool for committee accomplishment will, we feel, greatly enhance committee accomplishment. It is one of the simplest, most direct ways to begin a process of improved committee decision-making. For this to happen, however, the agenda maker must recognize that the agenda is a complex document which requires proper attention to structure, proper attention to the form of minutes, proper attention to the nature of reports, and proper attention to the very language in which the agenda is written. If all of these things occur, the agenda can become a vital tool for effective meetings. And remember, rather than using the traditional, or at least usual, agenda (beginning with reports, and having the key business left, often, till last), place the most important matters in the middle of the meeting, so that they can be completed by approximately the two-thirds point in the meeting. That will be a great help.

After Hank left, the meeting of the Social Planning Committee petered out. Bob Grey had been angry with Hank. "Who does he think he is, anyway?" Bob said to the group. "Everyone knows that it is important to have freedom from constraints." Bob had been the chair, and secretly felt chagrined at Hank's outburst. Not only was it something, he felt, of a personal criticism, but Hank was an influential man in town, personally respected, and he controlled important budget allocations as well. At that point, Peter Josephs spoke up. "Maybe Hank did have something of a point," he said. "Why don't we have a meeting and talk about our meetings." "Good," said Fran Fox. "But let's each send Bob a little note about what could be better first. Then he can see what suggestions and problems we have in common and make a sort of list." "Fine," Peter said. "And I'll call Hank and see if we can get him back on the track." People left feeling much better about their activity than they had over the past year.

NOTE

1. An example of an in-principle decision is a decision to look for an outside executive replacement rather than an inside one.

Chapter 6

TROUBLE-SHOOTING

As we talk with people about committee work, certain problems come up so often that it seems useful to discuss them in some detail.

What are some of these problems? Generally, they fall into three main categories:

- the improper choice of mechanics for the committee process
- the misalignment of committee types and functions
- the lack of evaluation and accountability mechanisms.

These are the most common difficulties encountered by committees. They come up repeatedly. We'll take them one at a time.

MECHANICS OF COMMITTEE PROCESS

By mechanics we mean those aspects of the committee process that make the committee work. While these mechanics are related to the agenda and the structure of the meeting, they can be handled separately. We will consider the following mechanics:

- attendance
- food
- the first meeting
- participation control
- taking minutes.

ATTENDANCE: How do we get people to attend meetings? To find the answer, we might do well to ask another question. How is it that people do not attend in the first place? All too often the answers suggest some peculiarity of the offender's personality. While this may occasionally be true, in the majority of cases looking through committee minutes, agenda, and modus operandi makes it clear why people do not attend. Procedures are sloppy, agendas are indistinct, there is no harmony of process, and no apparent order. Meetings seem to begin and end at will. Thus, when a member, particularly a thoughtful member, has to evaluate his or her time against the disappointing experience of the meeting itself, the meeting loses.

So we begin with the committee structure itself. We have made several suggestions, many of a tidying-up nature, that can make committee work more orderly and that emphasize keeping to declared goals. We suggested that you trim down reports, shape and focus discussion items, use the bell-curve structure. These kinds of changes streamline and rationalize the committee process. They often do wonders for the attendance. If people begin to say, "Well, things are really getting done now. It's worth coming to this meeting," but some still do not attend, it is time to look at the individual problems facing the member. Sometimes they are just too busy to attend.

Are there ways in which we can help members to contribute when attendance is impossible? Can we use the technique of remote participation in which the member is called, or is asked to call to give an opinion on the items before the group that day? Have we tried every possible way of reminding members of the meeting date and time? A two-media method of communication might include one contact by letter and another by phone. A written announcement might include a returnable card. We have found that the use of two reminders rather than one, each conveyed by different media, results in a clearer message and better attendance.

Finally, of course, you can explore with the member whether he or she is overcommitted. If that is the case, then you can offer to switch the member to an ex officio membership, or to a consultancy, or to some other role that takes advantage of the member's contribution but does not demand regular attendance.

RULES FOR
CORRECTING NONATTENDANCE

1. streamline the procedures
2. remote participation when needed
3. use two-media communication to remind them about attendance
4. find out if member is over committed and arrange for a different form of participation

FOOD: What about food at meetings? Our rule of thumb is simple, if extreme. *The less food at meetings, the more likely it is that something will get done.* Keep in mind that when we use the term meeting here, we are not talking about exploratory sessions, quasi-social sessions, preliminary discussions, and a whole range of other reasons why people get together. We are speaking of a committee meeting with an agenda to be followed, decisions to be made, and work to be brought along. Food is distracting: somebody crunches on the celery, or knocks over the milk reaching for a second helping of spaghetti, a plate slips onto someone's budget report, etc. The meeting process is interrupted with "pass the salt, please," "delicious prime rib," "can I have a second helping?" and so on. Food diverts a meeting. Turn food into a reward for good committee performance, not into an agenda item. Nothing is as pleasant as a good meal after a heavy morning's work. Coffee, however, is permissible, but take care about who *makes* the coffee and who *pays* for the coffee. Trivial as those items seem, they become sufficiently large to block committee progress simply by taking up time. Refreshment available at the break, on the other hand, is welcome. Remember, the less food, the more work.

RULES OF THUMB ABOUT FOOD

1. allow coffee
2. provide refreshments at breaktime
3. the less food, the more work
4. use food as reward, available only after, never during the meeting

THE FIRST MEETING: Perhaps no meeting is more important than the first meeting. We all know that first impressions of a class, of a professor, of a potential date, of a business partner have a lasting impact. The first meeting, too, is absolutely crucial in setting the mood and pace of the particular committee. If the chairman strolls in late and without apparent thought to the meeting beforehand, this conveys a lack of seriousness which is immediately picked up by the committee. Regardless of whether that impression is correct, it will stick. Getting a bad reputation is easier than shedding it.

For this reason, tremendous attention should be paid to all aspects of the first meeting, whether it is the committee's first, the chair's first, or the staffer's first meeting. Investment there will pay dividends later in quicker work and a smoother process. In particular, it is useful for the chair to take the opportunity to call each member of the committee to talk with him or her, however briefly (but privately), about his or her hopes, personal agenda for the committee, and potential areas of interest and contribution. Apart from being courteous, this discussion is an essential part of the chairperson's intelligence-gathering procedures. It provides a clear picture of a committee's potential competency, interests, and orientation.

RULES FOR
THE FIRST MEETING

1. contact members beforehand about their concerns
2. be prepared with an agenda
3. be on time
4. set the model for future meetings

PARTICIPATION CONTROL: How about the member who talks too much? We do have a lot of Tommy Talkalots in the world, yet we encourage them with vague agendas and by failing to be clear about what the topic of discussion is. We urge chairs and members to enforce rules of relevance and we stress that *both* the chair and the members must enforce them. Sometimes the members sit back and let the chair do all the work, secretly delighted that Tommy is "really giving it to him this time." It is impossible, though, to enforce such rules without topical focus. If, for example, a topic up for discussion is "the budget," then little can be introduced that does not relate to that massive topic.

Obviously, then, participation can be focused by writing more specific agenda items, through greater and better targeting of topics for discussion. Then, for example, the chair can ask Tommy Talkalot whether his point is for or against the item up for discussion. That kind of intervention on the chair's part is only legitimate, though, if that is clearly the activity required. Beyond that we encourage chairs to call upon the less vocal members before calling upon the talkative member. It is sometimes necessary, as everyone knows, to ask such a member to wait until others have had their turn, or to remind that person that he or she has already had a turn and others now need to take theirs. Generally speaking, the committee will support chair intervention if the chair is evenhanded and if it appears that this prerogative is not being used to simply silence views that are "out of synch" with the chair's.

The quiet member, of course, should be drawn out as much as the talkative member's output should be tempered. Direct questions about the quiet member's opinion on this or that are frequently helpful. Sometimes the chair or another member can take the opportunity to meet with a quiet member outside of the meeting, discern his or her views, and then ask whether or not to report the quiet member's views if the member him or herself does not wish to do so. Sometimes people are waiting to be asked. This kind of invitation is enough to get them rolling. Sometimes they are confused about matters but are embarrassed to say so. Great sensitivity is needed to find out why people are quiet. The different reasons one uncovers for this situation can lead to radically different modes of intervention.

RULES FOR
BETTER PARTICIPATION

1. emphasize the issue on agenda
2. focus on decisions to be reached
   or items to be clarified
3. target discussion
4. orchestrate comments
5. draw out silent members
6. temper overbearing members' output

See Exercise 13 (p. 108)

MINUTES: What should minutes be like? We favor content minutes, made up of brief paragraphs summarizing the different points of view with the decisions explicitly recorded. Any further or follow-up steps, including dates, reporting times, forward times, and so on, need to be explicitly noted there. PUT THE DECISIONS IN CAPS FOR EASY REFERENCE: Make the minutes easy to read in format terms and fairly brief. It is, of course, courteous to send copies of minutes to associates of the committee if something in the committee business relates to them, or if the minutes reflect their participation on some kind of guest basis.

Minutes should be agenda relevant. Avoid asides, irrelevancies, pieces of stage business which do not do anything except cloud the central point of discussion. Lean, crisp minutes, like lean, crisp reports, should always be the order of the day.

Who should take the minutes? Generally, the staff person assigned to the committee takes them, or the duty is rotated from member to member. In our view, it is not necessary that the secretary be the person who always takes minutes. If this were so, the secretary would rarely be able to participate. Consider the secretary as the board or committee archivist, the person who is responsible for keeping the records, for keeping a complete set of minutes, and, quite possibly, for issuing them after a rough draft has been received from the person who takes them.

RULES FOR
MANAGING MINUTES

1. take agenda-relevant content minutes
2. assign recording to staff, or rotate recording among members
3. free the secretary to function as keeper of records, archivist
4. share copies with key board/ committee associates

COMMITTEE FUNCTIONS AND TYPES

What exactly is a board, an ad hoc committee? How does a board differ from a commission?

The most important types of committees and groups are:

- the board
- the task force
- the ad hoc committee
- the standing committee
- the commission
- the advisory group.

We'll say a few words about each of the first five types of committees in this section and defer discussion of the advisory group to the next chapter. Each type performs distinctive functions.

What do we mean by "functions and types"? Most committees are not of a single "type." Most are predominantly one type, but perform other functions; and when they do, they partake of the characteristics of that type. Committee functions include the giving of advice, the making of decisions, the gathering of information, and so on.

THE BOARD: the board is a legally chartered, legally responsible, decision-making body. Its function is to make decisions. Its procedures, the processes it uses, and the expertise it takes should all be oriented toward that function. Boards are, or should be, known for the decisions they make, and should be able to make them after appropriate deliberative time. Postmature decisions (taking too long) and premature decisions (deciding too quickly) should be avoided.

THE TASK FORCE: Unfortunately, most of the groups called "task forces" are really "task farces." A task force is, or should be, a group of people with the resources (decisions, equipment, money, people) needed to carry out some assignment. A Red Cross Disaster Team is a good example. Almost all "task forces" are really advisory committees.

THE AD HOC/STANDING COMMITTEE: Ad hoc committees are the kind almost all committees should be—appointed for a specific mission, with a sunset provision, a given time in which they are expected to go out of existence. Standing committees, on the other hand, are ones which have a continual life. Sometimes assignments (of people or tasks) can be made on a time-lined basis to permanent committees. The reason we like ad hoc appointments, even where continual functions are involved, is that they permit a reassessment of new functions and memberships without giving offense.

COMMISSIONS: These groups are usually appointed to make decisions by some political authority (road commissions, Presidential commissions, etc.), and, as such, have a political cast to them. Commissions often issue reports and cast their decisions in the form of recommendations or policies which are to be followed up by others.

INFORMAL MEETINGS

What about informal meetings with friends? Can we also look at these? People tell us, "Your suggestions are fine, but surely not for a small church group or for a group of my friends." We could not disagree more. While it is certainly true that any set of rules needs to be applied with intelligence and discretion, we feel that informal groups where people know each other well are among the most dissatisfying to the members. Precisely because people know each other, they seem to take twice, three, or four times as long to accomplish something that strangers could do with dispatch. Partly, of course, this lengthened time can be explained by the multiplicity of agendas that always come up when friends get together. However, our attention has been drawn again and again to the lack of focus, the lack of detail planning, the lack of thoughtful preparation that characterizes more intimate committees. No physician would avoid giving a proper physical examination to someone just because he/she knew that person as a friend. Similarly, lawyers have a saying that a man who acts as his own attorney has a fool for a client. All these speak to the dangers of intimacy and lack of objectivity at crucial moments. What we suggest, then, is that one should use many of the procedures for orderly meetings as well as the prethinking and preplanning we have suggested in *The Essentials of Committee Management* and elsewhere. A little planning does not hurt. It can help a great deal, particularly in those groups where planning is thought to be unnecessary, and thus is nonexistent.

EVALUATION AND ACCOUNTABILITY

Now let us turn to evaluation and accountability. How is the committee to know whether or not its decisions were good? You can't answer that question without proper records because no one, yourself included, can remember what you have done. Foremost among them are minutes that are crisp and clean. Relevant documents should be attached to them. Appropriate revisions should be noted in those minutes. The findings of subcommittees should be communicated in writing. Together, these records provide the basis for the evaluation of explicitly recorded decisions.

When we evaluate a committee's functioning, we will not evaluate whether the coffee came on time or whether the meeting room was well ventilated. Certainly these are crucial. They are necessary but not sufficient conditions, or preconditions, for good decision-making. Rather, it is the decision itself that is to be evaluated. It is our suggestion that the minutes be culled toward the end of the year for a list of decisions that can be put into an annual or summary report.

It has been our experience that these decisions will fall into several areas of concern, that there seem to be some unifying themes. Decisions, then, can be organized by "theme," listed, and rated. We suggest a scheme for rating that uses standard academic marks, or grades—a, b, c, d, and f.

An "a" decision is one which seemed to improve the situation for all concerned, though not necessarily equally. A "b" decision is one in which there was overall improvement, but there were some important winners and losers. A "c" decision is one in which some ground was lost, but there continue to be some winners and some losers. The "c" decision is the typically partisan decision in which one says, "I'm going to get mine regardless of what it costs you or others." The "d" decision is one in which everyone is worse off than before the decision was made. An "f" decision is a "d" decision where the committee winds up being fired on top of it all.

Committees can develop other rating schemes. The only advantage in ours is that it takes a system we are used to using, puts it on one side of the paper, lists all the decisions on the other, and asks for an intelligent grading of the decisions that have been made. This scheme represents two improvements over anything else available. One is that it requires committees to do what they often do not do—list decisions. The process itself leads to evaluation. Second, it suggests that thoughtful judgment be applied, in retrospect, with the new information now available.

The annual review of committee activity is an essential part of planning for the next year. Frequently, one can get out a statement of operational goals framed in the first or second meeting, put that against the overall mission statement, and then look at the set of decisions taken and ask the question, "Overall, have we made any progress towards our goals, or have we not?" That kind of question is an essential one for the next round of committee activity. If it is asked, that next round will be even better than the previous one.

RULES ON HOW TO
EVALUATE

1. gather minutes/other
   documents
2. summarize and review
3. grade

The accountability aspect of committee and board life is hard, of course, to enforce. All too often, people are rewarded for bad performance with more committee assignments! This is best avoided, in our view, through the evaluation and grading procedure. Any procedure, really, will be fine, as long as it involves:

(1) systematic recording of decisions (which means making them in the first place!);
(2) a systematic assessment, after time has passed, of those decisions;

(3) a modification of committee procedure and member and chair prac-
    tice based upon those decisions.

Improvement, not punishment, is the goal to seek.

SUMMARY

This chapter reviews some of the areas of frustration frequently mentioned
by those in committee work. The mechanics of the process are examined:
improving attendance through better focus and improved communication,
limiting food, taking special care with the first meeting (to set pace and tone),
and developing efficient recording mechanisms. Several types of decision
groups are discussed: the board, the advisory group, the standing and ad hoc
committees, and the task force. While the advisory committee is discussed in
depth in the next chapter, we noted here that confusion in the purpose and
function of decision-making groups can have a negative effect on their
performance. Many "problems" can be handled with a little forethought and
planning.

Chapter 7

THE ADVISORY COMMITTEE

Sam and Ed walked out of the Occupational Health Advisory Committee Meeting in Capitol City. "Good Lord," said Ed. "To think we came all the way from University City for this!" "I know," said Sam. "I still can't believe it." What Sam and Ed were talking about related to the processes of the most recent meeting. Their group was to advise the new director of Occupational Health on a fresh, new state health plan. When they arrived, they saw secretaries wheeling typing chairs loaded with paper into the committee room. There were three to each chair, one pushing and two holding, since the stacks of paper were high. The director apologized, but said she could not get the report run off in time. The secretaries passed out page after page of this two-hundred-page report, and the committee members collated it. While that went on, a number of members were trying to do some private business involving funding with the director, each warily eyeing the others. Finally, the stuff was passed out, and the director said, "Well, why don't you take a few minutes to look this through, and then you can give me your advice." Sam at that point had indicated that it was impossible to do that, since they could not read it. The director said that she needed reaction right away, because she was seeing the Governor later in the day.

THE ADVISORY COMMITTEE

Although many of the roles and rules we have talked about should serve you well in most situations, they will need to be modified for various kinds of

AUTHOR'S NOTE: An early version of this chapter was prepared for use by the staff of the Michigan Department of Mental Health, whose comments and support are gratefully acknowledged.

committees. One of the most frequently misused committee types is the advisory committee. On the surface, its functions seem clear enough—the advisory committee's function is to give advice. But so frequently do we hear about its problems that we feel a specific chapter devoted to it is required.

The advisory committee often includes a fairly high status "advice seeker." This person, an executive of an agency, perhaps, is frequently the chair of the committee providing advice.[1] The chair/advisee may bring along assistants, secretaries, and so on. This immediately creates a situation in which the committee is overwhelmed by numbers and influence. It is very difficult, for example, for a member of an advisory committee to say something critical to a prominent advisee. It is even more difficult when that advisee is flanked by assistants, associates, and others in, perhaps, larger numbers even than the advisory committee membership itself. This is especially so when the advisee tosses out some fast-breaking, late-developing items for the committee to consider. Different members will comment now on this aspect, now on that. The advisee may conclude by saying, "Thank you very much. This has been most useful and most helpful."

This brief scenario illustrates almost all of the bad things that can happen at an advisory committee meeting. If we look at each in detail, it will help us formulate some rules with which we can manage advisory committee functions more adequately. The first thing to keep in mind is that the advisory committee should produce a coherent and intelligent piece of advice, carefully considered and acted upon by the committee as a whole. While ad hoc discussions on one or another issue can certainly be useful, informal discussions should in no way be thought of as substituting for a coherent advice package.

MISSION AND ROLE

The first rule for an advisory committee is to clarify its own functions. These tend to include one or more of the following:

- advice
- review
- approval.

Some advisory committees can give only advice to a designated advisee. Other advisory committees have some additional power because they must review certain materials—though not approve them—before action can be taken. For example, a state agency might be required by law to establish an advisory committee to review a development plan and comment on it before it can go forward. Seeing and commenting upon the development plan does not mean that the advisory committee must approve it. However, they do have power to refuse to see a particular plan, and in that way they can effectively block action.

Some advisory committees play an "advise and consent" role in which their approval is necessary. This ratification function gives the committee considerably more authority.

What differentiates advisory committees from, say, boards is that they do not make the decision. Their function is to comment intelligently on the decision made or to be made by others. The advisory committee is evaluated on the basis of its advice, not upon whether its advice is taken. Many advisory committees spend long hours lamenting that they have no "power," and seek to seduce, induce, or otherwise influence the advisee to do what the committee wants.

WRITTEN ADVICE

After the committee determines exactly what it can do and what it must do, it should require, as an operating norm, that all its advice be given in writing. That means that the advisory committee will review a concern, formulate views, and crystallize those views into majority or minority views. If appropriate, it will vote and communicate its advice in writing to the advisee. This advice must be the committee's collective judgment, not a series of independent, individual judgments. Each piece of advice conveyed to an advisee should have been voted upon by the committee. The advisee may be informed whether the vote was unanimous, whether there were substantial different points of view. Where significant differences exist, a minority report is quite legitimate. However, a majority report accompanied by some minority emendations is quite different from a hodge-podge of individual views. Following the rule of coherence is crucial.

RULES FOR
GETTING IT IN WRITING

1. review
2. formulate
3. crystallize
4. vote
5. communicate

AN EX OFFICIO ADVISEE

Regardless of the traditions in a given community, we feel strongly that no advisee should be chair of her or his own advisory committee. It is virtually impossible to exercise the role of chair appropriately when the objective is to get advice that is going to yourself. The advisee should always be an ex officio member, one who sometimes sits in to share information or provide explanation, and, of course, since advice will be put in writing, the advisee need not always be present to receive advice. Since advisees are usually relatively high status types, it is almost impossible to avoid contamination of the committee deliberations. Objective advice is often best given when discussion can occur without the advisee being there. Conclusions can be drawn and then be communicated thoughtfully in writing to the advisee for his or her own review and consideration.

WRITTEN RESPONSE

The advisory committee should always request its advisee to respond in writing. In this way, the advisory committee can know specifically what it was that the advisee did or did not like about the advice, what he or she found helpful or impossible to accept. Advisees, of course, will not be totally candid in all instances with their written responses. Some may not wish to provide them at all. Nonetheless, it is extremely helpful if this practice can be insisted on because it structures the interaction between the committee and the advisee in a particularly useful way. It answers the complaint that, "we never know why the advisee did (or did not) follow your advice." And it induces the advisee to be open and honest with the committee, clearly laying out the reasons for action.

ASSESSING ADVICE

Because many advisory committees are rarely expected to do much more than participate in "bull sessions," no group consensus is ever arrived at. The quality of the advice given is hard to assess. The advisory committee may not even know what advice it gave the advisee. If one presses the point and asks, "Look, you're an advisory committee to Mr. X, and I'm one of the constituent members of your group. I'd like to know what kinds of advice you're getting together to give X," the weaknesses of the "bull session" style of advisory committee activity become apparent. One never really knows what advice was given because there really was none.

On the other hand, if the written model is followed, the answer to that question is fairly straightforward. "Well, we have had a number of discussions, and they have crystallized into several pieces of advice. I would be happy to provide you with copies of our report if you would like to see it." The written advice and the response to that advice are essential to the committee's ability to evaluate itself. At the end of the year, several members of the committee should get together to review all their pieces of advice together with the responses to that advice. This will permit committees to look seriously at what they did as well as consider in depth the response they got, and to compare both.

The "bull session" is nevertheless useful when the committee is asked to share preliminary ideas that the advisee would like to try out. In effect, the advisory committee might have a dual focus: a long range focus that weighs activities of a more thoughtful nature, and a practical focus commenting on day-to-day ideas brought by its advisee. Some of these day-to-day issues will emerge as topics for a longer study. The real problem is how to keep these two very different types of agendas from interfering with each other. We recommend the split-agenda technique.

THE SPLIT AGENDA

The split agenda suggests dividing the committee meeting into two parts. The first part of the meeting considers the range of items and formulates written advice. During this period, the advisee need not always attend. By prescheduling, the advisee can be invited to attend approximately halfway through the meeting.

This does not really violate the nature of the agenda structure discussed earlier. The agenda structure can be used for the first half of the meeting. After the break, a "for discussion only" format in which the advisee is present provides opportunity for informal explanation and advice giving.

It is possible—and often desirable—to invite the advisee to comment on various kinds of ongoing matters as well. This can take place in two ways: through the oral meeting process which we just described, or by inviting the advisee to respond to a preliminary draft of the written piece of advice. In this way, one can get a feel for the advisee's position without becoming overinvolved.

GENERAL RULES FOR
AN ADVISORY COMMITTEE

1. give thoughtful collective
   advice
2. put advice in writing
3. request written response
4. meet independently for many
   of the deliberations
5. review work regularly
6. meet with and without
   advisee
7. check carefully for
   minority views

SUMMARY

Review the general rules listed above. These overall guidelines will
immensely improve the work of the advisory committee. People will feel
better about the committee; they will have a sense of achievement. They will
be able to see the effects of the advice that they have given because it is
written and because there will be, at least in some instances, written responses
to it.

Sinclair Westfield had also been at the meeting of the Mental Health
Advisory Committee. He was thinking, as he was driving home, about how
things could be made better. As a prominent physician, interested in the
public well-being of people in the state, he was troubled by the fact that the
advisory committee never seemed to get anything done. While today was
worse than usual, the meetings were usually less than useful. He made a note
to call Sam Cohen and Ed O'Brian that evening to see if they couldn't get
together and come up with some ideas for improvement.

N O T E

1. Of course, this is not always true. Sometimes the advisee is not a relatively high
status individual, and sometimes she or he is not chair. But these situations are common
enough to take note of them.

Chapter 8

DEVELOPING A PERSPECTIVE

This conclusion will seek to pull together some of the perspectives offered here and suggest some overall considerations for those interested in the board and committee process, recalling some of the material from the beginning of the book in a way that will suggest a perspective for the future on group decision-making and will help you frame your own ideas and outlook.

Better Quality Decisions are the Goal

First, we would like to emphasize that the goal of this book is to make people more aware of the group decision-making process and their roles in it. Use it to develop your own perspective. In turn, this awareness, it is hoped, will lead to better quality decisions. Decision quality is something which is all too rarely considered in thinking about the committee and board process. Yet that is what it is all about, really. We get together to make decisions. Naturally, if the process is as chaotic as it often seems (and is!), then those decisions will be good only due to chance. We believe that this process can be improved. Through preparation, forethought, and the application of selected techniques, the decision-making group can, initially, begin to make decisions. This right action in committee and board will, we are sure, amaze some and surprise others. Once decisions begin to be made, then the task of improving them can begin.

Personality of the Member is not the Main Cause of Trouble

Much of the time, we focus upon the personality of the member as one of the main causes of problems in committees. This diagnosis places blame squarely in the hands of an Arthur Angry, of a Tommy Talkalot. And there is a happy consistency with the American ethic of individualism. Surely, personality contributes something here. Yet, as we have emphasized in this volume, the committee process and the board process are group efforts. Blaming one person is like blaming one man on an assembly line for a car that does not run right. We need to look at the structure of the roles, the extent to which people know their roles, the extent to which they have role flexibility and can switch from one role to another, and so on. Once these elements are taken into account and we are satisfied that they have been improved, then work on one or two troublesome members can begin.

The Meeting is the End, not the Beginning, of a Process

All too often, people who think about ways to improve meetings begin their work *at* the meeting. That's like trying to prevent conception by talking with the unwanted child after he is born. Much work, as we suggest, needs to be done before the meeting begins. The committee and board process is like an iceberg, with the meeting as its tip. The direction that tip travels is dictated by the massive understructure of the iceberg; the way the meeting goes is similarly dictated by what has—or has not—gone on before. The meeting is the public performance of the committee, and one can look at what has been done before to see why that performance is a success or a bomb.

Planning and Preparation is a Process Which Frees, Not Constrains

American society is not planning oriented. As many observers have pointed out, we tend to play the "sleeping giant" role, waiting until some crisis or other develops before moving massively to do something about it. Whether it's family planning, social planning, urban planning, or board planning, we seem to find it hard. Somehow, planning gets identified with a restriction of opportunities. "Let's play it by ear" is a frequent phrase. "Conflict never hurt anyone; it clears the air" is another which comes up again and again. And there are times when one wants to work with a minimum of structure, or permit some conflict to clear the air. However, as a general rule, our experience suggests that conflict is often the result of confusion and lack of information, and that "playing it by ear" is not a sensible way for the committee/board orchestra to go. One gets cacophony, not a concert.

Planning and preparation, so that people know what to expect, and can prepare themselves for it, decreases the likelihood of poor decisions. Items in the agenda, such as "for discussion only" items, permit a time when discussion can be free flowing, but around preidentified topics. Reports are structures designed to highlight the matters to be decided and to suggest options.

Decision-making groups work best when they can build a decision structure from among a series of decision suggestions or decision elements based upon work done outside of the meeting. They are not good when they are required to operate in ways that do not give them the information required. Planning and preparation identifies these elements, develops alternatives, and provides, thereby, grist for the committee mill.

Conflict, is, of course, useful to a degree. However, conflict and tension need to be managed effectively, so that they do not become the primary elements within the group situation, so that the making of decisions does not become secondary. The agenda structure itself, through the scheduling of items in the bell-shaped curve way, provides a way for managing conflict. Indeed, it recognizes conflict, and suggests that for conflict to be effective, it must be handled at a period in the meeting when there is the physical energy, the psychological energy, and the attendance to process it.

Group Decision-Making Will Only Increase

Because demands for goods are increasing and resources are diminishing, the need for group decision-making can only increase in the years to come. Additionally, as problems become more complex and technical, as many different types of knowledge are required to solve them, then group decision-making will increase. And finally, since products are the result of many hands rather than a single pair of hands, the owners of those hands need to get together to talk about how the final product can be improved. It seems to us that a program of improving group decision-making structure and skill can only be helpful. Rather than looking at one more committee as an additional burden to take one away from "work" (which is always done alone), we should try a perspective in which such situations are seen as opportunities for improvement, and try, through these techniques and others, to maximize their utility, to make that next meeting not only worthwhile to you, but to others as well.

APPENDIX

Exercise 1: Rules for Effective Committees/Boards

Think of a committee or board you serve on. Then think about the following question in relationship to it.

1. How well do you and the members know the membership role there? Well? Poorly? A mix? Why?

   _____

   _____

   _____

2. Were the tasks structured on a preliminary basis? Yes? No? Why?

   _____

   _____

   _____

3. Did the group make good decisions? Poor decision? ANY decisions? Why?

   _____

   _____

   _____

   _____

Exercise 2: Rules for Committee Functions

Think about a board or committee on which you serve. With it in mind, consider which among the board/committee functions it might be fulfilling:

— to equalize participation in decision-making?

_____

_____

— to demonstrate preference?

_____

_____

— to represent social diversity?

_____

_____

— to express diverse opinions?

_____

_____

— to decide?

_____

_____

— to influence others?

_____

_____

How might these various functions compound decision-making difficulties?

_____

_____

Exercise 3: Rules for Maintaining Focus

Pick a recent meeting that you have attended. Now that you have called it back to your mind, think about the five rules for maintaining focus. See if you can answer the following questions.

1. Was there AGENDA INTEGRITY—were all scheduled items discussed? Were unscheduled items kept to a minimum? Was there an agenda in the first place?

   _____

   _____

   _____

2. Was there temporal integrity? Did the meeting begin and end on time?

   _____

   _____

   _____

3. Was the agenda set up so that the important information was available in advance (rule of halves)? Did it come out in time (rule of three quarters)?

   _____

   _____

   _____

4. Was the meeting run so that the most important items came in the middle third of the meeting?

   _____

   _____

   _____

   _____

Exercise 4: Rules for Membership

All too often we do not look into a potential membership or chairship too thoroughly. Later we find we are stuck. If we think about the manifest and latent aspects, we may become more knowledgeable members before we even get on to the committee. Think of a recent committee or board you were asked to chair, and think of one also that you were asked to join. With these in mind, think about the following rules with the (a) STATED, PUBLIC reasons (manifest ones) in mind, as well as the (b) UNSTATED, PRIVATE reasons (latent ones.)

Some examples of stated public reasons might be: they needed your skills, they needed your interest, no one else was as good, it would only take a little while, and so on. Some examples of unstated private reasons might be: they needed a woman (minority, person of a certain religious background, whatever); you were the only person who would accept; you are known as a strong (weak) person, and the appointing authority wanted to send a message to some group observing the process; etc.

1. What are the conditions for membership?
   (a) public, stated reasons (and conditions)

   _____

   _____

   _____

   (b) private, unstated reasons (and conditions)

   _____

   _____

   _____

2. What is the group's mandate?
   (a) public, stated mandate

   _____

   _____

   _____

   _____

   _____

   (b) private, unstated mandate

   _____

   _____

   _____

   _____

   _____

3. What is the meaning of membership?
   (a) public, stated meaning

   _____

   _____

   _____

   _____

   _____

   _____

   (b) private, unstated meaning

   _____

   _____

   _____

   _____

   _____

   _____

4. What is the meaning of acceptance (to you, to others)?
   (a) public, stated meaning

   _____

   _____

   _____

   _____

   _____

   _____

   _____

   (b) private, unstated meaning

   _____

   _____

   _____

   _____

   _____

   _____

Exercise 5: Running a Meeting

Think about the last time you were chair of a committee or board. Now that this setting is in mind, think about your behavior during that session, and answer the following questions about it.

1. Did you model (give, through your behavior, an example of desired behavior) committee behavior?

   _____

   _____

   _____

2. Did you try to bring together people of different political orientations (set 1), different types of ideas (set 2), and ideas and people (set 3)?

   _____

   _____

   _____

3. Did you preside in a neutral, statepersonly fashion, seeking to involve everyone and temper those overinvolved?

   _____

   _____

   _____

   _____

Exercise 6: Rules for a Committee Administrator

Thinking still of that recent meeting (from exercise 5), try to answer the following questions.

1. Did you get out the agenda? (and, thinking about the meeting in retrospect, was it adequate?)

   _____

   _____

   _____

2. Did you follow up on reports (and, in retrospect, did you do this sufficiently)?

   _____

   _____

   _____

3. Did you check on members' assignments (and, in retropsect, did you do this sufficiently)?

   _____

   _____

   _____

4. Did you set the stage for the meeting by having all the materials and room in readiness?

   _____

   _____

   _____

   _____

Exercise 7: Board and Committee Training

Think of a recent board or committee on which you have had membership, then answer the following questions.

1. Was some kind of preparation of members present? If not, what could have been done to establish such a program?

_____

_____

_____

_____

2. How could the principle of legitimacy for training have been established?

_____

_____

_____

_____

3. Was there a board or committee manual? If so, look at it in terms of some of the suggestions made here. If not, make a short outline of topics which you feel should be included.

_____

_____

_____

_____

_____

_____

Exercise 8: Rules for an Options Memo

Consider the sample memo:

Memo To:	Bea Sharpe, Chair, Compensation Committee
Memo From:	Sally Swingle, Staffer
Re:	Raise Policy Options

You asked me to consider what a raise policy might be. Various staffers have different views on what would be appropriate. I have talked with them, and also looked at other agencies, and have identified the following options:

(1) an across-the-board increase in dollars (this gives people differential percentage increases);
(2) an across-the-board increase in percentages (this gives people differential dollar increments);
(3) some mix (note that dollar increases benefit those earning lower salaries, percentage increases benefit those earning higher salaries).

In addition, there are various bases upon which any of the three principles might be used:

(a) merit, in which some measure of ability/contribution is used;
(b) seniority, in which some measure of organizational age is used;

My personal recommendation is to use a (1) and (a). I would be happy to discuss this with the committee at its convenience.

cc. committee members

Now, think of some recent situation in which you had a report. See if that information can be boiled down to as compact a memo as this one. Note the three parts: analysis, options (1-3; a, b), and recommendation.

_____

_____

_____

_____

_____

_____

Exercise 9: The Staffer Role

Think of a recent meeting where you had someone staff your committee (provide assistance to it). Did that person perform the following tasks?

Role	Performed: Yes or No	How well
1. inform/provide consultation		
2. give technical assistance		
3. stimulate committee activity		
4. promote committee function		
5. analyze choices		
6. develop strategies		
7. set meeting stage		
8. serve committee interests		

Think of some time when you might have had such a role. Which of these functions did you perform? How well do you think you performed them?

1. _____

2. _____

3. _____

4. _____

5. _____

6. _____

7. _____

8. _____

Exercise 10: The Executive

Think of a time you were on a board which had an executive. Did that person perform the following tasks?

	Performed:	
Role	*Yes or No*	*How well*

1. present a professional perspective _____
2. offer expertise where needed _____
3. keep board informed of policy issues _____
4. work sensitively with the board _____
5. offer development opportunities _____
6. work energetically with agency staff
   and between board and staff. _____

Think of some time when you might have had such a role. Which of these functions did you perform? How well do you think you performed them?

_____

_____

_____

_____

_____

_____

_____

Exercise 11: The Minutes

Select from your files a copy of a set of minutes from a recent meeting. Look at them from the perspective suggested in this volume. Do they:

1. report views without naming disputants?

_____

_____

_____

2. summarize debate?

_____

_____

_____

3. record action taken?

_____

_____

_____

4. categorize items under agenda headings of previous meeting?

_____

_____

_____

Exercise 12: The Agenda

Consider the bell-curve agenda format suggested in chapter 5. Now take out an agenda from some recent meeting you have attended. Look at the items, and, recalling the meeting, reorganize the items within the bell-curve format.

Original List Of Items	New List of Items in Bell-Curve Format

Now that you have done this, try your hand at some upcoming meeting's agenda and see how it works. (If you say to yourself, "But I don't have the items," then you know the importance of the rule of halves.)

_____

_____

_____

_____

Exercise 13: Rules for Better Participation

Think about a recent committee meeting you have attended. Review in your mind the level and quality of participation at that meeting. If your session was a typical one, about this point you'll be saying, "Oh, *that* meeting!" Think, now, about how participation could have been improved.

1. more emphasis on the agenda? (even getting one!)

2. more focus on decisions to be reached?

3. a better targeted discussion?

4. a better orchestration (sequence and appropriateness) of comments?

5. could silent members have been drawn out?

6. could overbearing members have been tempered?

_____

_____

7. are there other things which, in thinking it through, could have helped?

_____

_____

Now that you have this diagnosis in mind, think about what you could do in preparation for your next meeting which might be helpful.

_____

_____

REFERENCES

Books and Articles

AUERBACH, A. J. (1961) "Aspirations of power people and agency goals." Social Work 6 (January): 66-73.

COHEN, M. D. and J. G. MARCH (1974) Leadership and Ambiguity. New York: McGraw-Hill.

COX, F. et al. [eds.] (1977) Tactics and Techniques of Community Practice. Itasca, IL: Peacock.

DUSING, R. (1977) You and I Have Simply Got to Stop Meeting This Way. New York: American Management Association.

GIERMAK, E. (1960) "Individualism vs. the committee process." Advanced Management 25 (December): 16-19.

GOFFMAN, E. (1959) The Presentation of Self in Everyday Life. New York: Doubleday.

PRICE, J. (1963) "The impact of governing boards on organizational effectiveness and morale." Administrative Science Quarterly 8 (December): 361-378.

REISCHAUER, E. O. (1978) The Japanese. Cambridge, MA: Harvard University Press.

TROPMAN, J., H. JOHNSON, and E. TROPMAN (1979) The Essentials of Committee Management. Chicago: Nelson-Hall.

New Journal

Directors and Boards: The Journal of Corporation Action, 1621 Brookside Rd., McLean, VA. 22101.

Film

Meetings, Bloody Meetings. Xicom/Video Arts, Sterling Forest, Tuxedo, NY 10987.

READER FEEDBACK

We would like to know what you think about committees and boards. Could you take a moment and fill out this feedback sheet, and drop it to John E. Tropman, School of Social Work, University of Michigan, Ann Arbor, MI 48109?

1. What is your reaction to the modern board and committee? Do you think they serve a useful purpose?

_____

_____

_____

2. How might they be improved?

_____

_____

_____

3. How did you like this book? What were the things you liked the best? What were the things you liked least?

_____

_____

_____

4. Have you had any special board/committee experience that you would share with us?

_____

_____

_____

_____

ABOUT THE AUTHOR

JOHN E. TROPMAN is Professor of Social Work at the School of Social Work, University of Michigan, and Research Scientist at the Institute of Gerontology of the University of Michigan and Wayne State University. He holds an undergraduate degree from Oberlin College, a Social Work Degree from the University of Chicago, and a Ph.D. in Social Work and Sociology from the University of Michigan. Interested in policy formation and implementation, and community organization, Tropman has written numerous articles in these areas. He developed a course in "Board, Task Force and Committee Management" which is taught at the University of Michigan. As both consultant and trainer, he has assisted numerous groups in the United States and Canada to improve their committee functioning.